PRAISE FOR THE THINKING REVOLUTION

The Thinking Revolution is a comprehensive guide to what really makes human beings tick. Dene Stuart takes us on a journey of discovery whilst dispelling numerous misconceptions en route. Skilfully weaving together centuries of thinking about thinking, and grounding it in the real world, this book will provide you with the tools and insight needed to recognise your own true potential and plot your course towards it.

Chris Shaw – Head of Culture and Communication, Advantage Business Partnerships Ltd

Working with Dene, I have seen my business, and indeed myself, transform. *The Thinking Revolution* is a powerful tool to help you overcome your fears and find the courage to achieve what you want.

Nicole Speller – Director: Churchmill Accountants and Business Advisors

The Thinking Revolution is a book that captures and précises the content of many of the great psychologists and authors. [Dene brings] together accepted and qualified knowledge published by others and presents it in a way that makes it easy for the reader to understand. Dene isn't reinventing the wheel, he's repainting it.

Mary Bell – Managing Director, UR Beautiful

Dene shares his hard-won wisdom in an engaging, honest and ultimately useful way. He weaves three golden threads through these pages to guide and develop our own thinking revolution. He prefers to ask us important questions rather than supply easy answers himself… I never once felt that Dene was talking at me, and that made the reading all the more thought-provoking.

Richard Maybury – CEO Attitude Solutions, Institute of Directors HR and L&D, Ambassador for Surrey

Finding your route to success is rare, setting yourself free to be the best version of yourself is even rarer. Dene delivers how to accomplish both. Highly recommended thought leadership!

Marty Lucas – Entrepreneur, Author, Columnist

This book will increase your awareness and push your buttons about the real needs behind your goals. And in doing so, will be the only personal development book you will ever need.

Tony Brown – The Soulmate Specialist and author of *Why Your Perfect Partner Can't Find You!*

This book is a pure joy because it takes you on a journey; it is well-researched, written and even makes you laugh in between.

Rhys Marc Photis – MD & Founder of Global Performance Improvement Ltd

A book I would be very happy to recommend. I can't see how the reader wouldn't be absorbed and encouraged to take the first step to positive change.

Peter McDonnell – CEO, Cordoba Group

[In] *The Thinking Revolution* [Dene] uniquely offers the reader the means to think for success. Told with personal charm and perspective this is so much more than other self-help books, it's a product of passion, knowledge and great thought applied.

Ben Hart – Founding partner, Atmosphere and Professor of Marketing, Hult International Business School

You should consider this book to be the operating manual for you. Read it thoroughly, do the hard yards, and notice the improvement in you.

Neil Botten – Management Consultant and Non-Executive Director at The Institute of Continuing Professional Development

Rarely does an author bare their heart and soul in a business book. Dene shares great advice for better thinking and better doing for the reader to achieve a more balanced and successful life and work environment.

Daryl Woodhouse – Founder and Head of Strategy and Leadership, Advantage Business Partnerships Ltd

An uplifting and empowering read with stimulating new ideas and an easy to follow conversational style.

Jenny Simnett – Managing Director, People in Places Ltd

Dene has an extraordinary way of bringing to life theories and methodology that ordinarily would be difficult to digest. *The Thinking Revolution* has indeed caused a revolution within me, my thinking and what is now possible. Thank you Dene!

Gozi Halima Nwachukwu – Executive Coach, Founder of the Soul Summit London

THE THINKING REVOLUTION

UNLEASH THE FULL POWER OF YOUR MIND

DENE STUART

RedDoor

Published by RedDoor
www.reddoorpublishing.com

ISBN 978-1-910453-16-2

A CIP catalogue record for this book is available from the
British Library

Cover design: Rawshock Design

Typesetting: Tutis Innovative E-Solutions Pte. Ltd

Printed in Great Britain by Bell and Bain Ltd, Glasgow

CONTENTS

Foreword   **vi**

Introduction   **1**

The Applied Principles of Success   7

Have You Ever Thought About Your Thinking?   11

What Makes You Tick   26

The Anatomy of Success   33

Understanding Awareness   45

Resourcefulness   59

Needs   73

Wisdom   102

Understanding The Journey   139

Positivity and Negativity   153

How to Use The Thinking Revolution   162

Creating Your Centre of Gravity   170

Renew   178

The Final Curtain   193

Further Reading   **198**

Acknowledgements   **201**

About the Author   **202**

FOREWORD

I first met Dene at a local networking meeting, and was immediately impressed with his quiet composure and his knowledge of the subject of mindfulness and emotional intelligence.

I had worked at a high level in both the Probation Service and NHS before opening my own business. Initially I required Dene to work specifically with my son who was working for me as my manager, but was struggling with his self-confidence and lack of business acumen. This was a particular concern for me as the long-term plan was for my son to run the business when I retired; I needed to have confidence that this would be feasible in the long-term and my hope was that Dene would be able to help my son grow from thinking of himself as an employee, to believing in himself as a business owner.

Dene worked with him on a fortnightly basis and was able to challenge my son about some of his beliefs and attitudes. It was immediately obvious that Dene was able to communicate and change behaviours in a way that radically altered my son's attitude to life and, more importantly, the way the business could be run by him.

Since working with Dene my son has transformed the way he thinks, has developed his self-confidence and I now feel confident that my business has an exciting future beyond me, giving me the security of knowing I can now look forward to my retirement.

In his latest book, Dene reveals the unique strategies and processes he introduced to my son with such great effect, and I know they will be an asset to anyone who wants, or needs to develop themselves or their business.

This book develops the principles Dene first put forward in *ResourcefulMe* and takes them to a new level and depth in such a way that we can all, by following his ideas and teachings, cultivate and improve our own effectiveness and achieve the success we are all looking for in our lives.

Pauline Herring
Proprietor, Everycare Central Surrey Ltd
Surrey, England, 2016

INTRODUCTION

'What did you learn today? What mistake did you make that taught you something?'

Carol Dweck

The yeti burst in through the front door and the snow swept in with it. We were screaming and frightened as it came towards us.

'Run!' shouted John.

'I can't,' I replied. 'I'm too scared.'

I was about nine or ten years old when I wrote this story for my English homework.

I felt really excited as I handed it to my teacher. I'd written about three sides in my exercise book, the most I'd ever produced, and in exactly the same style, or so I thought then, as the books I was reading at the time. Biggles, the Hardy Boys, the Famous Five, the Secret Seven. I thought my teacher would be really pleased because I'd written in such a grown-up way.

What followed was to shape my life significantly.

I received the worst mark I'd ever had for a piece of homework. I can only recall my teacher remarking: 'Don't you know how to write?' which left me feeling devastated. It seemed this was the worst story he had ever read, even though I thought I'd done everything he'd asked for. Yes, my handwriting was pretty awful, but I was so excited by my story idea that I couldn't write slowly enough for it to be neat and tidy.

When I got home my mum went through my exercise books, as she always did, and discovered the teacher's comments. Now, although she was a very loving mum who only wanted the best for me, that day she was to say something that would change my life: 'Your trouble is you've got no imagination.'

1

Being so young, and having been brought up to obey the adult figures in my life, my only way to cope with this judgement of me was to agree and to deny my own imagination. From that point I decided to focus on studies, such as maths and the sciences, that were non-subjective, meaning that I could only ever be right or wrong. Never again would my mark depend on the opinion of the teacher. By the time I was twelve my path was set and I had already closed my mind to many possibilities in life.

I didn't discover, until I read *Mindset* by Carol Dweck when I was in my early fifties, just how profoundly this childhood experience had affected my path in life. Carol is one of the most influential thinkers in psychology and a professor at Stanford University in the US. She developed a theory that there are two types of people, those with a growth mindset and those who have a fixed mindset. People with a growth mindset like challenges and are open to the learning that comes with failing and getting things wrong, and those with a fixed mindset are the opposite. They are not only closed to the learning that comes with making mistakes, but they tend to react as if it is a commentary on their personal abilities and a judgement about them as people.

This was just one of the many light-bulb moments I have had in the past few years.

I had been one of those fixed mindset people. What was more important to me was the mark at the end of the exercise, the approval I would get from my teachers and my parents, and this was to go on into my working life as I looked for approval from my employers.

This mindset was a major factor contributing to the collapse of my marriage and after twenty years of family life, I found myself living in a flat alone while I tried to rebuild the relationship with my children. How could I have got it all so wrong? How could I have misunderstood myself? But more importantly, how could I have misunderstood life so much? I entered what can only be described as a state of grief and mourning as I started to question my value as a human being.

One of the most important insights that came to me was that I had been living in fear, of many things as it turned out, but most importantly of the fear of failure. Through this period I started a period of study and learning and discovered the work of Carl Jung. One of his sayings is: 'There is no coming to consciousness without pain.'

What I was to discover is the process of coming to consciousness involves accepting personal responsibility for your own life, and requires the shedding of inherited beliefs and values and the development of your own. There is no age barrier to this process, although the later it happens the more painful it can be as you acknowledge the years that you have spent disconnected from your natural power.

Why do we need a thinking revolution?

There is a famous Buddhist saying: 'When the student is ready the teacher appears.'

At the age of fifty-two I began to discover all of this amazing information in the form of classic works ranging from Tao Te Ching to Stephen Covey's *The 7 Habits of Highly Effective People*. This knowledge had been around for millennia, it has been refined and reformed by various thinkers, philosophers, theologists and scientists, but I just hadn't noticed it. That's not true. I did see it but I thought it was a load of old hogwash. My fixed mindset couldn't allow me to see the value of personal development. But now the penny really did begin to drop. I was the one who had been closed to all of the learning that was out there. It was available to me all the time and any time I could have turned to it. But your eyes will never see what your mind doesn't want them to.

Many people resist personal development, believing it is tantamount to admitting weakness. I was well into middle age before I grasped its true value. In fact, investing in personal development is an indication that you value yourself. I regard it as the best money that I have ever spent on myself and it has led to my only lasting regret: that I didn't do it earlier.

Natural ability or developed potential?

Some people seem to rise naturally to the top of their tree. You might think of the Richard Bransons, Bill Gates, Steve Jobs of the world, and yet when you read their stories there are always other people they met along the way who helped them take their next step. Successful people use their inner resourcefulness to fulfil their needs, and having strong mentors is generally vital to the process. Their success happened for many reasons but not least because they were very good at what they did and, as importantly, they had a clear vision of what they wanted to achieve.

Understanding the spiritual gap

As I opened my mind and became ready and open to learn, I began to understand the great thinkers (when the student is ready the master appears). For the first time the link between spirituality and personal development and success became clear to me. I realised that it was possible to be spiritual outside of the context of organised religion.

For some this might seem obvious, but for me it was like a doorway into a new world and a new way of thinking. I started to read books I had laughed at in the past like *The Road Less Travelled* by M Scott Peck, in which he discusses his experiences as a psychotherapist and his route towards spirituality. As my reading diversified I began to see connections between the old spiritual thinkers – Buddha, Lao Tzu, Confucius, Aristotle, Socrates and Plato – and modern spiritual thinkers like Deepak Chopra, Gandhi and Gyalwang Drukpa. I was discovering positive psychology. Suddenly I found myself reading about neuroscience and discovering concepts like the continual creation and destruction of neural pathways. This led me to the works of scientists such as Daniel Amen and Bruce Lipton. The coming together of science and philosophy made complete sense to me.

The genesis of *The Thinking Revolution*

By now, I had been made redundant for the second time and I was facing the prospect of an uncertain future. The industry I'd worked in was in serious decline. It was time for me to make that jump and put into practice everything that I had been studying for the previous two years. So I committed to creating a business where people like me could come for the support, help and guidance they needed to fulfil their natural potential and pursue their inherent success.

It was only when I allowed the spiritual perspective into my life and learned about emotional intelligence that my perspective began to change. For the first time I started to see the big gulf between the person I thought I was and the way other people saw me.

There's a question used in the recruitment business when assessing candidates: 'Does this person really have ten years' experience or has he had one year's experience ten times?' It was hard for me to admit to myself, but I was the latter. I'd kept on repeating the same mistakes, bound up in my own thinking and fixed mindset, not able to learn the lessons that the universe was presenting to me, and therefore not able to take advantage of the opportunities the universe was offering at the same time.

Someone once said that a 'leopard can't change its spots', and they were right; but only if the person in question has a fixed mindset. When you have a growth mindset you have real choice and your perspective of the world takes on a whole new dimension.

My future was looking more uncertain than at any other time and yet somehow the extreme anxiety I had been feeling about that lack of control was dissipating. I was to experience the truth of this quote from Goethe: 'At the moment of commitment the entire universe conspires to assist you.'

I was starting to feel more at ease; with myself, with other people, family, friends and new business associates. Even so, everywhere I seemed to look was a particularly infuriating statement that is at the centre of just about every personal development programme: 'The answer lies within you.'

Why didn't any of these books and these programmes have the balls to come out and say what the answer was?

And then I met Vicki, who had just started her own publishing company, and was looking for new projects. It was through her vision that I ended up publishing my book, *ResourcefulMe* about our innate resourcefulness and how we can tap into it.

Buoyed with new energy, I started getting speaking opportunities. This led to new challenges as I had to develop my skills in this area.

By now I was following the work of Sidra Jafri, an intuitive healer. She introduced me to David Hawkins and his research into energetic states: this is the idea that we resonate with people who vibrate (have an energetic state) at our level. You may have heard this described as 'like attracts like'. Now it made sense to me why some people liked my work and why some people didn't, but more importantly I was OK with that. My need to be right all the time was disappearing.

I began to research theories about human needs. I was puzzled by the fact that if needs are what we have in common, why do we have different priorities, interests and motivations? I was to see it's because we all have a different experience of the world. Finally, I developed a model for my own personal development and coaching programme, as follows:

We apply our resourcefulness to try and fulfil our needs using our wisdom. Resourcefulness – needs – wisdom. (Serendipity was to play its hand here: If you take the first two letters of resourcefulness and needs and combine them with the first letter of wisdom you get *renew*.) More on this later.

The last part of the puzzle

I had discovered Daniel Pink on TED a few years previously and loved his line: 'There's a gap between what science knows and what business does.' It spoke to my experience working in the corporate world and led me to read his book *'A Whole New Mind'*. Here his core idea was that because the world is changing so quickly we are going to need new skills to remain employable and productive in, what he called, this new conceptual age.

This led me to the following thought, the ascent of man might therefore look like this:

1. The Stone Age
2. The Iron Age
3. The Bronze Age
4. The Agricultural Revolution
5. The Industrial Revolution
6. The Information Revolution
7. The Thinking Revolution

The objective of my book, *The Thinking Revolution,* is to bring an understanding of the unconscious forces that determine the direction your life is currently taking, so that you can become master of your destiny. When you can master the three key elements of your resourcefulness, your needs, and your wisdom and you understand the nature of your journey through life, you will be best equipped to achieve success in your life, whatever that success may be.

The Applied Principles of Success

'There is nothing either good or bad but thinking makes it so.'
William Shakespeare

'The mind is everything. What you think you become.'
Buddha

Some people seem to be able to tap into their intuitive success and live lives of purpose, meaning and joy. This doesn't mean they don't encounter difficulties along the way or that life presents them with an easy path, but they somehow seem more connected to a way of going about life that leads them to achieve what they want.

Others work hard but true success always seems out of their grasp. Some persevere, others give up and settle for a life of frustration. A small minority turn to crime as the only way they can see of making any material gain.

There have been many books published about success. By and large they have been written by people who have studied the methods by which other people became successful – and while this is useful you need to be able to determine the way in which you can become successful. Emulating the success of others is a good strategy but there comes a point when you have to work out how to create your own success.

I have written this book *for everyone who thinks they are capable of more than they are currently giving to the world.*

(Please review that last sentence. It does not say *for everyone who thinks they should be getting more from the world.*)

The mind versus the brain

Throughout this book I will make a distinction between the mind and the brain. That's because they are not the same. We all have a brain that functions biologically in a similar way, but we all have different minds.

To explain this more fully I have written *The Beginner's Guide to The Brain, The Mind and Thinking*, available at *http://thethinkingrevolution.com/beginners-guide/*

The four mindsets

There are four mindsets which you must be aware of. It is essential for you to nurture and maintain two of them for as long as you live. The other two you must try to banish. There is no halfway house because the four cannot live together.

They are:

1. The growth mindset
2. The fixed mindset (these are the creation of Carol Dweck and her research into what makes people successful)
3. The creative mindset, a natural expression of the life force that exists within each and every one us
4. The entitled mindset, that believes hard work should be rewarded.

So you are clear, the mindsets that you must have in order to maximise your happiness and sense of fulfilment are Growth and Creative. The mindsets you should eliminate are Fixed and Entitled.

You might feel some resistance to the descriptions you read in the diagram on page 9, which is an indication that you have that mindset. If you wish to become truly successful the first step is to recognise your resistance and then acknowledge it.

It is unlikely that you only have the symptoms described in one of the boxes. You can probably recognise the feelings associated in two or even three of the boxes.

If you want things to be different in your life – if you want to achieve more and get better results – you have to do things differently from now on. And the only way to do things differently is to think differently.

	Fixed	Growth
C r e a t i v e	If you have a **Fixed And Creative** mindset you will experience the following symptoms: Your feelings will be that people do not appreciate your ideas and that they are always rejected. You will also feel you are not given the chance to explain your ideas. Desired outcome: To get others to think the way you do.	If you have a **Growth And Creative** mindset you will experience the following: This mindset is tolerant, it embraces difference and sees growth as the opportunity to learn how to bring your natural creativity to the world in a way that the world is willing to and wants to reward. Desired outcome: to give your creative energy to the world.
E n t i t l e d	If you have a **Fixed And Entitled** mindset you will experience the following symptoms: Your feelings will be that people do not appreciate or value you and you are resentful of their lack of appreciation. Desired outcome: to receive praise and recognition.	If you have a **Growth And Entitled** mindset you will experience the following symptoms: Your feelings will be that you are growing as a person, that you are becoming more responsible and capable of taking on more responsibility yet this is not recognised or rewarded. This leads you to feel resentment and frustration. Desired outcome: To be given status.
Mindset	Fixed	Growth

The principles behind *The Thinking Revolution*

Throughout the course of this book we will unravel the ideas on the next page, doing exercises along the way. My hope is that by the end of the process you will have had your own thinking revolution and will have gained a dynamic new perspective on your life.

Consider the following statements:

- Your beliefs about the world are a result of your life experiences.
- What you learn from your experiences is dependent on your mindset: fixed or growth; entitled or creative.
- Growth will always occur but can be negative or positive depending on your mindset.
- Negativity is the self-protective, dominant way of the mind and has to be actively resisted.
- Negativity undermines positivity when the two exist together in one person.
- Success is a journey that can only start when your centre of gravity (your centre of gravity is the place in your mind where your beliefs about what is possible are held) is aligned with your natural talent or creativity, the expression of the life force through you.
- Natural talent is not enough to create success; it has to be supported by your resourcefulness.
- Your ultimate creativity expresses itself when your natural talent has been developed to mastery.
- Your resourcefulness can only be developed through regular use and faith, otherwise known as self-belief.
- Your motivation comes from your innate drive to fulfil your needs.
- Your ability to fulfil your needs is a consequence of your self-belief in your resourcefulness and your wisdom.
- Your wisdom is a function of your understanding of natural law (a body of principles that are considered to be inherent in nature and have universal application), your beliefs and your values.
- Success is only achieved when you have fulfilled your needs without preventing anyone else from satisfying theirs.
- Achieving one success is not an end in itself, but the beginning of a new journey.

Have You Ever Thought About Your Thinking?

'Very little is needed to make a happy life; it is all within yourself, in your way of thinking.'

Marcus Aurelius

'We cannot solve our problems with the same thinking we used when we created them.'

Albert Einstein

Humans have been thinking about thinking since we started to think. We've come to call this philosophy and we've even given it a technical term: metacognition (or thinking about thinking).

Let's start at the very beginning: why do we think at all?

Many scientists have made it their life's work to try and get inside the minds of other animals because it gives us insight into why human beings do the things we do. We know that there are various levels of intelligence just by watching animals in their native habitats. There can be very few people who haven't been fascinated by one of David Attenborough's amazing films showing the hunting strategies of a pack of lions or a bask of crocodiles. What these animals have in common is a survival instinct and an unpredictable future. It is by no means certain that the hunters will make a kill, or that their prey will survive long enough to reach their feeding grounds to satisfy their own hunger.

We can't know the emotions that these animals feel in their fight for survival, but what we can see is that the fundamental driving force of human thinking and activity is to remove the uncertainty of our existence.

Our human abilities have enabled us to get out of the cycle of survival in which other animals exist, but not to escape it entirely. At some point we will die, but we put a huge amount of our energy into trying to extend that end point as far as possible. The investment in health services and medical research of all developed economies is astronomical, aimed at creating cures and overcoming disabilities that would have seen our ancestors die off at a much younger age.

Consider how much of your mental and material resources you invest in order to take uncertainty out of your life. Every insurance policy you have, your pension, your marriage, your choice of career – all intended to remove the uncertainty from your life.

One of the biggest factors affecting mental health today is the increased uncertainty in the area of job security. Careers in public service and the corporate sector used to ensure a job for life and a gold-plated pension but this is no longer the case; and, as a result, work-related stress has seen an inexorable rise. Outside of this framework of employment lies the route of the individual: the entrepreneur, sportsman, musician, actor. To succeed they have to thrive on uncertainty and they are able to do this because they think of it differently.

The generation now coming through to adulthood, so-called Generation Z, born between 1980 and 2000, are rejecting the old ways of thinking because they cannot see the same level of certainty in the future as their parents. The world seems to have a lot more to offer, but the level of uncertainty has increased massively and it is driving a change in our behaviour.

We will do amazing things to reduce uncertainty; for example, we will work very long hours if we think our jobs are at risk; we can become manipulative in our relationships if they feel unstable, or we might choose a life partner who is not in harmony with our values to avoid the uncertainty of being alone. Take a few minutes to think about how you feel towards the uncertainty in your life. What choices have you made to reduce it?

'You're just like your dad'

I have been told this for most of my life. My father had been a very successful businessman, intelligent, witty and charming, but like all people he was a multifaceted character and that meant there were aspects to his personality that were less appealing. I came to associate the phrase with these less appealing characteristics.

Being of fixed mindset, and because I didn't like the negative aspects of my dad's personality, I resolved to never be like him. Because of the way the brain and mind work together, when you choose not to be or do something your brain is focused on the thing you don't want to be, and perversely it can bring out the very behaviour you don't want. So it was with me.

Think of a time you had a crucial meeting with your boss, or the date you had with the boy or girl of your dreams, and beforehand you thought: 'I really don't want to mess this up.' And then you do.

Our brain and mind really is a perverse combination. Most people never think about the way they think. I didn't. And yet it is only in understanding the way you think that you can develop the skills necessary to learn from your experiences and realise the full potential that exists naturally within you.

So let's start at the very beginning.

Why do we think?

Any creature with a brain thinks; or does it? Creatures like starfish don't have brains but function very effectively. Ants have brains, they form colonies and they take different roles within the colony and they work together to create some of the most sophisticated structures in the world. Complete with natural air-conditioning systems. Are they thinking or are their brains just control mechanisms?

If you're wondering what this has to do with you: how many times have you said to yourself or someone else, 'That's just the way I am. I can't do anything about it.'

Is your brain controlling you? Or are you in control of your brain?

At the most basic level of the human brain is the brain stem: this can keep us alive and breathing and is the store of our most primal instincts. It is only when all signs of activity have gone in this part of the brain that doctors are prepared to announce death. This level of brain is quite frequently referred to as the reptilian or lizard brain.

The next level is the limbic system and this is where higher brain functions such as emotions are generated. The limbic system is present in other animals such as mammals.

The prefrontal cortex is the part where our human characteristics come from and what lifts us above all other life forms.

So coming back to the question: why do we think?

At the most basic level we think in order to survive and to reproduce our species. So how much has your thinking moved on from this level?

Survival nowadays, particularly in the developed world, requires a level of knowledge and learning way beyond that which people even fifty years ago could imagine. The days of mass unskilled jobs are pretty much gone. Even if the job itself might not appear to require much functional skill, for example the coffee-shop barista, the companies that employ them need to have people with interpersonal skills so that customers have a pleasant experience and come back again.

Daniel Pink captured this evolution in his book *A Whole New Mind*. He believes that the jobs and careers of the future are going to require a different way of thinking in what he calls the conceptual age. Job creation is going to come in areas such as design (creating something beautiful), storytelling (being able to create a good narrative), symphony (the ability to cross boundaries and connect the dots), empathy (understanding what makes people tick), play (turning the serious into fun), and meaning (the need to deal with the big issues facing the planet). Escaping from thinking will no longer be an option because even the lowliest jobs will require new thinking skills.

Understanding your emotions

The brain creates emotional responses in our minds according to the stimuli it receives through our five senses, and then filters these sensory inputs into the conscious thinking part of our brain. The two most commonly referenced parts of the brain that work as filters are the amygdala and the reticular activating system. There are many others, for example the fusiform gyrus that enables us to recognise faces.

In very simplistic terms, your brain uses your beliefs and values as the database against which it judges what sort of emotional response to create. If you believe big dogs are scary and dangerous, seeing one will create a fear reaction within you. If you think they are loveable it will create a warm feeling instead. If one of your key values is loyalty and a friend doesn't invite you to their birthday party, your brain may create feelings of anger or jealousy or rejection.

These reactions occur in fractions of seconds before our conscious brain can kick into gear. It's only after we've had the emotional response to the stimulus that we then start thinking about what just happened. *Our thinking always follows our feelings* when the stimulus is an external one.

Because humans have the ability to imagine, we can create internal stimuli that also trigger emotional reactions. This is when we can start to tie ourselves into emotional knots.

It is no coincidence that emotional intelligence has been connected with success in all aspects of life, but there are a couple of key common misconceptions about it. Emotional intelligence is not about controlling your emotions, but rather the process by which you raise your awareness of them and hence your ability to manage your response to any situation. It is also about developing the skill to recognise the emotional state of someone else so you can more appropriately choose your response and so create better communications and relationships. Well-developed emotional intelligence gives you the freedom to choose.

My wake-up call came after I had lost my temper with my wife yet again. I had been an angry person for many years. I had grown up in an angry house and it had rubbed off on me. Of course when you're in the picture it's very difficult to see the picture. I had upset her very deeply; she couldn't understand how I could get so angry and it created a breach of her trust that I was never able to repair. As I was forced to face this aspect of my personality I made a conscious decision to think about it. It would have been easy to justify my behaviour by accusing her of provoking me, but I knew that wasn't the answer.

I realised I had been angry for most of my life, but I had never needed to confront it before. This time I knew that if I didn't confront that inner demon I would have no chance of saving my marriage. I wasn't to know at the time, but it was already too late. I had witnessed things in my world that angered me all the time. What I didn't understand was that I had unconsciously programmed my mind to search out the aspects that would trigger an anger reaction in me.

When I realised that my anger was a choice, I also realised that I could make different choices. I didn't have to see the world through angry eyes any more and I could choose different filters. I could see the world through happy eyes, optimistic eyes, loving eyes. After I had had this revelation, I made it my goal to change the choices I was making. But although I now chose to see the world through a different lens, it didn't stop me feeling the emotion of anger.

Anger is one of the deepest and most primal emotions we have. It is a safety mechanism. Anger helps us summon up our physical strength and it sharpens our mental faculties in a crisis. Have you noticed that your physical strength goes through the roof when you are really angry or that cutting remark is on the tip of your tongue just when you want to let rip?

Emotional intelligence is not about the removal of your emotions, but your *awareness* of them. It also concerns the ability to choose whether your thoughts and then behaviours are influenced by your emotions. This is the space of true empowerment: when you are in control of how you think, you can also be in charge of how you behave.

My dad had a saying: 'You should never be rude to anyone accidentally'. The more I have studied thinking and emotions, the less I can see the need to be rude to anyone.

Impulses

Have you ever thought about the expression 'acting on impulse'? When we act on impulse we jump from emotion to action, missing out thought. An impulse is not a habitual behaviour and can seem out of character.

Impulsive behaviour in itself is not necessarily good or bad and for many is the spice of life. It can create the feeling of living in the moment, but impulsiveness can also disrupt stable relationships if it becomes too frequent. Our relationships depend on predictability, whether they are with our loved ones, friends or colleagues. They have developed into relationships because of the predictability we've learned to expect.

Understanding your impulses is a key element of emotional intelligence.

A better survival strategy

The timeline of human evolution has been marked by our development of technologies. Over time, societies have created ever-more complex technologies that require even greater collaboration between people.

Until a few hundred years ago, the great leaps of discovery that took us forward were attributed to one person. You might think of Archimedes discovering his principle for determining the volume of an object circa 250 BC, or Newton explaining gravity in the late seventeenth century, or Lavoisier discovering oxygen in 1778. This pattern of individual discovery and invention carries through until the early 1900s when technology becomes too complicated for one person to have a breakthrough without collaborating with others – for example, Crick and Watson's explanation of DNA.

Nowadays new discoveries involve whole teams simply because of the complexity of the science. This has been mirrored in the evolution of the workplace which depends on continual innovation. When you need people to deliver creativity and thinking skills, you have to create the environment that will enable them to do it.

Understanding our own emotions is the key to self-awareness, and it is through this self-awareness that we develop sensitivity to the needs of others. This allows for the creation of successful relationships that are essential for any thriving community or organisation. A high level of emotional intelligence is becoming the marker of many successful organisations.

For example, the culture of a trading floor on the stock market will have a completely different feel to the environment of a hospice caring for the long-term sick. Emotional intelligence does not judge either to be good or bad but recognises that different types of people will thrive in the different environments.

Instinct

An instinct could be described as an inborn pattern of behaviour, something you don't need to learn – it happens naturally, without you thinking about it. In fact, there are instincts we are born with and there are patterns of behaviour that we learn over time until they become our instinctive responses.

A loud bang will startle a newborn baby and may even make it cry. But over time and exposure to enough loud bangs where nothing bad is associated with the noise, the startle will be taken away and the baby will no longer jump. You can see this in other animals, for example rabbits grazing by the side of the road, because they have learnt there is no threat as long as the traffic keeps moving. They only scatter if a car stops.

I was working with one client whose job was to manage the schedules of staff who had to deliver services to clients in their homes at specified times. She was dependent on the staff turning up on time. The normal vagaries with which businesses have to deal with their employees, such as illness, childcare issues etc., had a much greater impact on her than most businesses because she had to find alternatives, usually at short notice, which could be very stressful. Over time she had built a habitual response to the inevitable phone calls that came in on a daily basis. The habit was a very visual and vocal expression of the stress she was feeling and in extremes would manifest as bad language and aggressive gestures like slamming the phone down and banging her chair into her desk in frustration. She was unaware of how habitual this behaviour had become. It had developed into her instinctive behaviour, even when she encountered a problem that was relatively easy to solve. She was also oblivious to the effect she was having on the other people in the office.

Luckily she was open to working with me to develop her awareness of these behaviours. With newfound awareness came embarrassment as she realised how other people were seeing her and the effect she was having on them. This illustrates one of the principles of Carl Jung on which *The Thinking Revolution* is based: 'There is no coming to consciousness without pain.'

In a world where success depends on your ability to work with other people, this level of self-awareness is now an imperative.

This unconscious development of instinctive behaviours can be corrosive to all relationships. It can happen between work colleagues, parents and children and it very often develops between husband and wife, which over time can lead to big resentments.

It is the bringing of your instinctive reactions to events into the conscious mind that marks a thinking revolution and it illustrates another key principle of Jung's: 'Until you make the unconscious conscious, it will direct your life and you will call it fate.'

Exercise

What instinctive reactions do you have?

Do these reactions serve you?

How do you think other people see you at work? How do you see yourself?

Intuition

Intuition has a long history of discussion that can be traced back to the early Greek philosophers, and deep roots in Eastern cultures and religions, and is the single biggest reason we live in the type of society we do today.

It can be described as the ability to acquire knowledge or believe in the efficacy of an action without the use of reason or evidence to justify your belief. Other terms for it are gut feeling, hunch or inspiration. It is unverifiable, which makes it an uncomfortable approach for modern businesses.

In some ways it is our intuition that determines the path we take in life and the sense of happiness we feel. Many people end up feeling deeply unhappy with their lives because they did not follow their intuitive feelings but took what appeared to be a safer option.

The best example of intuition I can think of is often attributed to Henry Ford: 'If I had asked my customers what they wanted they would have said – faster horses.' Ford was driven by his intuition to create a car that could be mass-produced and was affordable.

Other examples of great intuitive leaps in business include:

Bill Gates – a computer on every desk. At a time when people accessed one centralised computer through their desk screen, this was a huge leap of thinking.

Steve Jobs – a computer that looked stylish and user-friendly that would ultimately make computers appealing for everyone.

Coco Chanel – The little black dress

Intuition plays an incredibly important role in our society but our education system is founded on the idea of giving people the knowledge they need to function effectively in society, and the concept of intuition is not on the curriculum.

Success could be described as the times that our intuition was right and failure as the times when our intuition was wrong.

It is in these moments of intuitive failure that our mindset determines what we learn. With a growth and creative mindset we can learn that a given combination of actions didn't work and look to try another. With a fixed and entitled mindset we are more likely to learn that we aren't cut out for that activity and give up.

One of the most spectacular examples of this was Steve Jobs' intuition that touchscreen mobile phones that used apps would be the future. The chief executive of BlackBerry ignored this, staking his reputation on the technology that had made them the powerhouse of the mobile phone industry. Job's intuition was right and BlackBerry's CEO was wrong as witnessed by the results enjoyed by the two companies. Our intuition occurs in all aspects of our lives: in the bright idea for a present for your partner, in coming up with a great way to spend the day with your children, how to solve an issue at work or choosing the destination for your next holiday.

The problem is we are never taught how to use our intuition. In fact, using your intuition is an essential quality in progressing in your career. Your intuition tells you what to do next. Your intuition is the point where your experience and knowledge and a problem that needs solving come together.

Because intuition can create big leaps in our thinking, it can also be the catalyst for triggering fears. Intuitive leaps may take you to an unfamiliar place because they come from your mind associating different ideas and creating something new, which can be scary. It is why most people don't follow their intuition. We know there are consequences to everything we do and it is the fear of these consequences that hold us back from following our intuition.

Insight

Insight is the realisation of why things happen the way they do, the linking of an effect to a cause. Psychologists say insight occurs when a solution to a problem presents itself quickly and without warning.

Insight is the result of a series of previously unconnected ideas and thoughts being connected through an unconscious process of thinking that is given time and space to occur.

Einstein captured this idea of insight as a process: 'It's not that I'm so smart, I just stay with problems longer.'

Reasoning and logical thinking

Reasoning and logical thinking is the ability to link facts and experiences together. There are many different ways of seeing the world and therefore what seems logical to you may not seem logical to me. Our logicality is linked to our personal beliefs and values. Our humanity often comes from the fact that we do not do things that are totally logical. Any fans of *Star Trek* will recognise this difference between Mr Spock and just about everyone he deals with. What follows are just a few of the ways in which our logical thinking goes out of the door when we make decisions:

(You will see the term heuristic used here. It is used to describe the process by which our brains take shortcuts to reach decisions. Enabling us to reach decisions quickly, which we can live with, rather than go through the very long process of collecting all possible information and analysing it before coming to a perfect decision. If you think about it, you use this method of thinking all the time but might never have known what to call it.)

- The affect heuristic: when the mood you are in affects the decision you make. You probably use this method of thinking most of the time.
- Anchoring: where exposure to related information influences the way you make a decision. You see this used in advertising all the time, for example, 'was £150, now only £99'.
- Availability heuristic: this refers to our inclination to make a decision based on the latest information we have. Think about a time you've reacted in the heat of the moment because of something you've just been told!
- Choice overload: Barry Schwartz wrote a whole book about this, *The Paradox of Choice*. He identified 'maximisers' who are not satisfied until they have reviewed all the options to make the optimal decision, and 'satisficers' who are happy with making a good enough choice. A maximiser might spend an hour going to lots of different shops just to save £5.
- Commitment heuristic: our continued commitment towards a decision, despite new evidence that the decision was not in our best interests. (Think of BlackBerry's CEO.)
- Confirmation bias: we are more accepting of evidence that supports the decision we want to make, than evidence that goes against it. This is why many managers and business owners appoint 'yes people' to their teams.
- Decision fatigue: we just get tired of having to make decisions and start to make bad ones as a result.
- Decoy effect: another trick used in advertising. Given a choice between two options, you will make the choice that appears best for you. When a third option is added you will make the choice according to the comparison with the third option. This may not be the best option for you.
- Endowment effect: we overvalue what we own compared to its true market value. This is true for physical things and also for our ideas and beliefs.

- Framing effect: the way options are worded will affect the decisions we make by distorting the way we view the situation. For example: if I want you to manage a situation with Joe, an employee at work, and start off by briefing you that 'Joe's a difficult character' you will go into your meeting with Joe in a different frame of mind than if I had said to you, 'Joe's having a difficult time but he's really trying hard to turn it around.'
- Halo effect: if someone we value uses a product it therefore means it must be good!
- Hedonic adaptation: when we tire of our standard of living. Think about the times you have had a promotion and salary increase. It doesn't take long before the novelty wears off and it ceases to be satisfying enough.
- Licensing effect: when you give yourself permission to do something bad because you've just done something good. For example, having a large piece of cake because you have just completed a 5k run.
- Optimism bias: we are generally programmed to overestimate the likelihood of positive outcomes over negative. It was the conscious application of this belief that allowed the organisers of the 2012 London Olympics to organise the facilities on time.
- Peak end rule: we remember the extremes of our experiences, whether this is the pain following an operation or the enjoyment of a meal. Patients will remember short but very sharp pain as being harder to endure than a lower level of pain that lasts for a longer period. In good restaurants desserts are always spectacular and luscious because they are the last memory you take away of your meal. Entertainers always leave enough for an encore to give the audience a really memorable end to the show.
- Reciprocity: we feel the need to return in equal measure something that we have been given.
- Scarcity heuristic: we value what is rare more highly than something that is readily available.

The Nobel Prize winner Daniel Kahneman captured these idiosyncrasies in his book *Thinking, Fast and Slow*. He claims we have two aspects to our mind, the fast and the slow.

The fast-thinking part is a necessary evolutionary development aimed at helping us survive and recognise dangerous situations quickly and react accordingly. It is driven by our emotions and doesn't take any conscious effort.

The slow-thinking part has enabled us to develop our societies and cultures. It is hard to engage, takes conscious effort and it is effortful to maintain.

The human brain evolved at a time when life was much simpler and when the choices we had to make were less complicated, but our brains haven't evolved significantly since. So sometimes we make decisions from our fast mind when we should be using our slow mind and this is why we end up making illogical decisions.

Rationality

Rationality is the quality or state of being reasonable. Rationality is the way our beliefs and values align with our actions or behaviours.

A rational perspective may suggest that a certain course of action is the right one, but our beliefs can override that thinking. This is best illustrated by people whose strong religious beliefs cause them to refuse certain medical treatments even when their life or the lives of their dependents may be at stake, and this raises moral and ethical questions when parents refuse treatments for their children.

When I was being treated for my cancer I never ceased to be amazed, as I walked to the hospital from the car park, to see patients in their pyjamas and dressing gowns with their drug bags in tow, still pumping the life-saving drugs into their cancer-ridden bodies, standing outside to have a cigarette. As fast as they were being treated they were helping to undo their treatment with the consumption of another toxic cigarette. It is amazing how often we do things that are irrational but they make sense to us at the time.

Levels of consciousness

Consciousness is used to describe our level of awareness of what is going on in the world. In some ways it is the drive to understand consciousness that has driven human endeavour almost from the beginning of civilisation.

Eastern spiritualism evolved the idea of seven chakras as an understanding of consciousness:

1. The crown chakra. Top of the head, represents connection to spirituality.
2. The third-eye chakra. The forehead between the eyes, represents thinking, imagination, intuition and wisdom.
3. Throat chakra. Throat, represents communication, self-expression, centre of truth.
4. Heart chakra. Centre of chest above the heart, represents love, joy, inner peace.
5. Solar plexus chakra. Upper abdomen, represents self-worth, confidence and self-esteem.
6. Sacral chakra. Two inches below the naval, represents abundance, wellbeing, pleasure, sexuality.
7. Root chakra. Base of spine, represents survival.

But there are many different definitions of consciousness, ranging from the medical to spirituality.

I have found it useful to think of consciousness in the following way:

Subconscious: this is the level of brain activity that runs the automatic physical systems in your body such as your breathing, heartbeat, digestion, hormone secretion and nerve impulses that are going on every microsecond. We wouldn't be able to survive if we had to consciously think about activating these systems.

Unconscious: this thinking guides our behaviours but we are not aware of it. Whether it's crying while watching a film, getting angry with your boss, or falling in love with your partner, these reactions are unconscious. If you've ever tried to explain a joke you will know that it loses its humour. This effect also happens when you try to explain emotions such as anger.

Conscious: the thinking that we do at a very conscious level, governed by the prefrontal cortex in the brain. Seeing an empty milk bottle in the fridge will prompt the thought that you need to go to the supermarket.

Super-conscious: This is the point where you become aware that something might happen. You can't be sure what but it reveals itself as a nagging feeling. You might say it's where intuition and insight exist. In his book *The Art of Learning* chess grandmaster and martial arts champion Josh Waitzkin describes the heightened levels of awareness that he experienced in moments of high concentration when playing chess and competing in martial arts, which enabled him to outmanoeuvre his opponents.

It's not about self-analysis

Thinking about your thinking is not about self-analysis. It is about becoming aware that the way you think has many different aspects to it. You don't need to understand all of the physical, chemical and scientific reasons why your brain works, or the way your thinking is created. When you know that your thinking has many aspects to it you can begin to recognise when you are thinking in a certain way.

What Makes You Tick

'What lies behind us and what lies before us are tiny matters compared to what lies within us.'

Ralph Waldo Emerson

At a surface level you know what foods you like, the type of people you enjoy mixing with, the products you like to buy, the men or women you find attractive, etc.

Knowing what makes you tick is about getting under the skin of these surface likes and dislikes to understand why. It is in the understanding of why that you start to develop self-awareness.

What makes you tick is more formally known as motivation, or why we do the things we do. Just as there are natural laws that keep the moon orbiting the earth and the earth orbiting the sun, there are natural laws that determine your motivation. We like to be seen as individuals but we also like to have communal interests. When communal interests create conformity, some people feel uncomfortable and for others this is a comfort blanket. We see this at play in all aspects of life, from the schools that parents want their children to go to, to the clubs and societies people join to find kinship, and to the associations that people form to build the bridges of trust that will allow their businesses to flourish. The freedom to be motivated by whatever 'turns you on' is a fundamental principle of most developed economies.

Some people have absolute clarity about what they want and it gives them direction and energy in their lives. For others the picture is not so clear and they spend a great deal of time searching for their passion.

Know thyself

Know thyself was inscribed on the Temple of Apollo at Delphi 3,000 years ago. It was the Ancient Greek version of knowing what makes you tick. It is a call to self-awareness and comes from a school of philosophical thinking that is still influential to this day.

For all of the scientific advances we have made and the social benefits that have come from those advances, we are still essentially searching for the same idyll. Historically there have always been two classes of people: those with money and power and those without. The search for meaning and fulfilment has always been associated with those who had the means to give the time to this pursuit. For the rest, their time was taken up with ensuring they had a roof over their heads and food on the table. This started to change with the growth of the middle classes during the industrial revolution, the beginning of the concept of a career for the masses which we now have today.

A career is much more than earning a good salary. You only have to think of any job interview you have attended. When asked the fateful question, 'Why do you want to work here?' the answer 'Because I need the money' is a guarantee of a short interview. Employers want to know that you are passionate about your role and the organisation you want to work for. It is about engagement, fulfilment and wellbeing.

Organisations have to go well beyond financial packages and provide a climate in which people will thrive. And yet, survey after survey shows that the majority of people do not feel fulfilled by the jobs they do. We may have the inalienable right to pursue happiness but we don't seem to be very good at doing it.

At the older end of the age spectrum, people know they are likely to live longer and they want to live meaningful and rich lives; the idea of retirement is anathema to many people.

However, there is one thing that remains as true today as it did in the times of Plato, Buddha and Lao Tzu. Knowing what makes you tick will help you to live a purposeful and meaningful life.

Motivation

The study of human society is the study of motivation. Every step of progress that human society has made has come from the inner drive of a person or a group of people who wanted to do, create or get something new.

The scientific study of motivation is relatively new. Freud famously studied human drives and his theories emerged in the early nineteenth century. In 1932 William McDougall published *The Energies of Men: A Study of the*

Fundamentals of Dynamic Psychology. He listed eighteen human needs that drive our behaviours. In 1954, Abraham Maslow published his seminal work *Motivation and Personality* from which his idea of a hierarchy of needs would transform the way in which motivation was thought of and studied.

Many have followed on from Maslow. The whole field of psychology is essentially the study of why the heck we do the things we do, with sub-themes covering how can we do them better and how can we stop doing the stupid things we do.

Values and beliefs

Our values are the criteria by which we set the standards we wish to live by and they are part of the mechanism by which we recognise people who are similar and different to ourselves. It is my experience that it is the difference in personal values that drives much of the misunderstanding and breakdown in communication between individuals and groups of people.

This is also true for our beliefs. Our beliefs can be divided into two areas: what we believe to be true about ourselves and what we believe to be true about the world. As we grow older these beliefs have a bigger impact on the decisions we make and the way we view the opportunities that life presents to us. As we become older our beliefs become more fixed in our minds unless we maintain a growth mindset. The more we 'know' the more it limits our options and the opportunities we see in life.

It is our values and beliefs more than any other factor that determine whether we see opportunity and then act on it.

What are your values?

Most people only consider their values when placed in a situation of moral dilemma. For example: do you allow an employee to get away with a sub-standard performance because you are friends outside of work? Do you help your daughter to get a better grade in her homework? Do you confront your partner because he leaves the toilet seat up even though he knows it really annoys you? (Not all dilemmas have to come from big issues.)

When you have clarity on your values it will help you to understand why you might have areas of conflict with others. If your highest value is loyalty but your best friend's is hard work, you should not be surprised when she turns up late to your birthday party because of a rush job at the office. Because of your values you may see it as a comment on how much she values your friendship, but she felt she had no choice because getting the job done had to take precedence. If understanding and compassion are important values to you, then you will be able to see your friend's point of view and not allow the situation to damage to your friendship. But if one of your highest values is an eye for an eye, you may look for the next opportunity to pay your friend back for what you perceive as her disloyalty.

By understanding your own values and accepting that no one, not even your partner or best friend, will hold exactly the same values as you, you can start to minimise the conflict in your life.

In knowing your values and understanding where you are not living to them you reduce the internal conflict you experience. This internal conflict is very draining of energy and motivation and we spend time wrestling with ourselves, conflicted in the decisions and actions we should take.

Reducing conflict with others only comes when you can accept that they are allowed to hold their values in exactly the same way that you can hold yours. If you cannot accept this then you will forever be disappointed by the behaviours of people who do not hold the same values as you.

The anger exercise

To identify your true values think of situations that make you angry. For example, I used to get very angry when people I knew didn't return phone calls in a timely manner. When I sat down and considered why that was, I realised that respect is one of my higher values. I like to respect other people and therefore when I feel that they don't respect me it makes me angry.

If you're not a person that gets angry easily, you can do this exercise from the opposite perspective. Think of situations that make you feel happy or good inside. These situations will be a reflection of when people have shown you the personal qualities that you value. Repeat this exercise until you have a list of at least ten values, but you will be holding considerably more in your unconscious mind. Values can usually be described in one or two words, for example; loyalty, compassion, hard working and honesty. However it is important that you do not look at a list and make a choice. This will not connect you to your values. The anger exercise is the best one I know but it requires effort. The results, however, are worth it.

I came to realise that there is generally a gap between the values people write down on their list, and the way they actually behave. When we write out our list of values it is as if we are writing a description of the selves we would like to be. Some people can become very down on themselves as they acknowledge this gap, but this is the wrong diagnosis. What this exercise reveals is how ineffectively they are fulfilling the need that sits behind the value.

Using the example of the value of hard work:

Let's assume you work hard and consider that you give good value to your employer for the salary they pay you. But sitting not far away is someone who gets paid pretty much the same as you but they don't work as hard and they're not as diligent. How does that make you feel? Probably pretty irritable behind the scenes. So what need of yours isn't being met in this situation? Maybe it is simply your need for recognition that is not being met. A lack of recognition can also breach our need for justice.

Bear in mind that the relationship between your values and your needs is driving the way you think and feel and behave.

What are your beliefs?

Our beliefs about ourselves, and the world, start to develop from the day we are born, guided by our parents and other influencers in those early years. Carol Dweck saw these beliefs at play in her research in schools. It was her insight into the way beliefs affect our mindset that became the subject of her work. Dweck saw the effects in all areas of life – in education, in business, on the sports field and in relationships.

She showed that what you believe about yourself to be true will influence the choices you make and therefore the path you will travel and the opportunities you will have in life. She seems to have proved Henry Ford's comment: 'Whether you think you can or you can't, you're right.'

Where does intelligence fit in to this?

How you view your own intelligence has a major influence on how you display your intelligence, which impacts on the choices you make in life. If you don't believe you are intelligent you will not put yourself in situations where your intelligence will be tested. There are many stories of successful entrepreneurs, sports stars, politicians and musicians who became super-successful but whose school reports suggested that they might go on to struggle in life. But there is a difference between intelligence and education. Education is no guarantee of intelligence, and intelligence is no guarantee of an education.

Howard Gardner, author of *Multiple Intelligences: A New Horizon*, suggested that there are nine different types of intelligence:

1. Intelligence in language (verbal skills and the sensitivity to the sounds, meanings and rhythms of words)
2. Intelligence in logic and mathematics (the ability to think conceptually and abstractly, and the capacity to see logical and numerical patterns)
3. Intelligence in 3D space and vision (the capacity to think in images and pictures, to visualise accurately and abstractly)
4. Intelligence in body and movement (the ability to control one's body movements and to handle objects skilfully)
5. Intelligence in music (the ability to produce and appreciate melody, rhythm, pitch and timbre)
6. Intelligence in relationships (the capacity to detect and respond appropriately to the moods, motivations and desires of others)
7. Intelligence of the self (the capacity to be self-aware and in tune with inner feelings, values, beliefs and thinking processes)
8. Intelligence of nature (the ability to recognise and categorise plants, animals and other objects in nature)
9. Intelligence of philosophy (the sensitivity and capacity to tackle deep questions about human existence such as: What is the meaning of life? Why do we die? How did we get here?)

Even thinking about intelligence in this way can open your mind to new ways of thinking. Whether you believe yourself to be intelligent or not is one of the most influential aspects of how you think. It can propel you forward or hold you back.

Understanding the four energies

In his groundbreaking book *The 7 Habits of Highly Effective People*, Stephen Covey introduced the idea of the four energies to the business world.

- Physical energy: to be effective in anything we do we have to be physically able to do it.
- Emotional energy: knowing how your emotions affect your energy levels is vitally important in understanding how other people see you. You will most likely know the feeling of feeling energised through experiencing emotions such as anger and fear but afterwards feeling deflated as your mind and body recovers from the adrenalin surge and other hormones that flood the body in these moments. Hopefully you will also know the energy that flows from feeling courageous or enthusiastic. The term 'flow' was coined by the positive psychology movement to describe the feeling of being fully engaged in what you're doing, to the point where you become lost in it and lose track of time. Children are naturals at this.
- Mental energy: your ability to maintain a learning mindset in a rapidly changing world.
- Spiritual energy: your spiritual energy will keep you going when everything else seems to be falling apart. It is where faith lives. Ultimately it is our faith in ourselves that determines whether we achieve the things we set out to do.

If you don't understand consciously what makes you tick, you can't know what to do to fulfil your needs Auschwitz survivor Viktor Frankl said: 'Between stimulus and response there is a space. In that space is our power to choose our response. In our response lies our growth and our freedom.'

What makes you tick is what causes you to react to the world the way you do. How can you be free to choose your response to life if you don't know why you react to the slings and arrows of outrageous fortune?

The Anatomy of Success

'If you can imagine it, you can achieve it. If you can dream it, you can become it.'

William Arthur Ward

Wealth and Success

I would like to offer this definition of success: a state that is reached when you discover your unique potential to create wealth; and that true wealth is anything material or mental that adds to the total level of positivity in the world.

You only have to look at the activities of wealthy people and analyse what they do with their wealth to see if they are true wealth creators or merely money accumulators. Wealth creators like Richard Branson, Bill Gates, Warren Buffett and Mark Zuckerberg create opportunities for other people to become successful and therefore wealthy. One of the ways they do this is by donating large proportions of their money to social causes but the other way is by allowing others the opportunity to discover and develop their creativity and therefore their success and therefore their wealth.

Have you ever really thought about what success means to you? Have you ever committed those thoughts to paper? If so, you are in a minority. One of the reasons we don't do this is our fear of failure. But you can't have success without failure. Failure rides alongside success like a passenger on a long journey. The trick is to make sure that failure doesn't become the driver.

At an individual level, we in the West have a fundamental misunderstanding of what success really is, and a lack of understanding of how to achieve it. Success is a function of doing something new in life and it is always bound up with change. Plus, it usually only comes to our attention after the event. There is no news value on reporting the achievements of a struggling inventor or musician, artist or scientist. So we don't hear about the thousands of hours that they put into learning, practising and trial and error to get to a point that they have something that works. Even then we are unlikely to hear about them if that individual success is not translated into money or media acclaim. We usually have no concept of the trials and tribulations of those who achieve their success until they have published their biographies.

The consequence of this limiting way of viewing success is that it creates a limited view of success: that it is only for the few, those ul-tra-dedicated, focused people who sacrifice many pleasures to achieve their ambitions.

What are dreams?

Whether your ambition is to get married at eighteen and raise a loving family or to become a sports star and compete in the Olympics, or it is to become a successful executive or entrepreneur you are holding a dream.

(This is not about the dreams we have in our sleep. I'm referring to our vision of how we would like life to be in the future.)

Dreams are part of our uniquely human gift of imagination. When Descartes said: 'I think therefore I am' he should have added: 'I dream, therefore I am human.'

My bet is that now we are talking about dreams some emotional reaction has been triggered in your mind. If you are like most people, that reaction would have been negative as you mulled over the dreams you have had that you haven't achieved yet (forgetting about the ones that you have). The idea that dreaming is a useful skill is drummed out of us at a very early age in school, because we are taught that dreaming is not practical. Apart from my ill-fated essay attempt I cannot remember a single lesson at school where I was encouraged to allow my imagination to run free.

The fact is, the world we live in has been shaped by people who had dreams: that we would no longer die from disease; that we would have safe, secure homes to live in; that we would not die from starvation and would not be subject to the brutality of others.

If you had a dream and you knew that if you followed that path you would be guaranteed to succeed, it would no longer be a dream. You would march on with certainty, being able to justify to yourself, your family and your friends that you were not chasing a dream but the certainty of success, and they would all applaud you.

It is the prospect of failure that causes us to classify our ideas and wishes as dreams. But what if your mind only ever gave you dreams that you were capable of fulfilling?

A dream is not something that you can achieve right now with the skills and abilities you currently possess. That's the point about a dream: it represents a vision of something you have yet to achieve and you can only do that through change and growth. *You have to become the person capable of achieving that dream.*

Now we are coming to the nub of this issue.

Our dreams represent the difference between who we are today and who we want to be, and sometimes that gap is too big and too difficult for us to contemplate and so we dismiss the dream.

Success comes from understanding your dreams and recognising that you also have to embrace the possibility of failure.

Exercise
List the dreams you have had in the past that you have achieved, however small.
What are your current dreams?

Living to your potential

Have you ever had the feeling that you have more potential than you are using in your life? If so you are among the vast majority of people at work today. There has been study after study showing that up to 85 per cent of people are dissatisfied in the jobs they do. (This also applies to many people who run their own businesses.) This is because we have a native sense of what we are capable of and yet we tend to work in places that are not geared up to help us achieve our potential.

The organisations we work for strike a bargain with us. They give us money on a regular basis in return for us doing what the organisation needs to survive and thrive. The organisation is only interested in helping you to achieve your potential if it sees you as necessary for its own survival, so what we are left with are bosses whose job it is to determine whether you have what it takes, and their idea of your potential is likely to be very different to yours.

Your dream is your unconscious mind's way of revealing to you the gap between what you are doing currently and what you could be doing.

A process for success

One of the problems we have with success is the programming we are steeped in through our culture. We only see success when it has come to fruition, we only recognise success when it is visible, like an apple hanging from the tree. We don't acknowledge that success is represented by the germination of the seed that eventually starts to grow into a tree and the time it takes for the tree to mature to the point that it has blossoms that can be germinated and then become apples.

We just see the apples and say how lucky that tree is to have apples, I wish I could have apples like that. Well, you can. It comes from recognising the process and accepting that success very rarely happens overnight; it can take a long time to happen.

Let's call the fruit on the tree 'big success'. Big success can only be seen as a consequence of many, many small successes.

The seed has to fall on fertile ground, the ground has to be of the right nature to support the germination of the seed, when germinated the sprout has to be strong enough to withstand the onslaught of predators and disease, and it has to do this until the branches are strong enough to bear the weight of the fruits it has produced.

The process of success is the story of growth, and the story of your personal success follows this pattern. The only difference between us and the apple tree is that we have the ability to imagine how our fruits are going to be. We can lie in bed and envisage a future filled with different fruits.

The problem we have is not imagining the fruit; it is choosing the right fruit that we want to grow.

The problem with our thinking

Because of the way our schools, universities, television companies, newspapers and radio stations are organised, we are conditioned to expect big success from the beginning.

The reason why shows like *The X Factor* and *Britain's Got Talent* are so successful is because of the promise of the immediate success it offers and the vicarious pleasure that the audience gets from watching those who make the journey. Over the course of a few short months of hard work it is possible for an unknown to become a national star and enjoy the fame and fortune that goes with that. In fact, many of the contestants will have worked long and hard for years to develop their talents before appearing on those shows.

Understanding what success means to you is a fundamental part of the process. When you don't recognise and celebrate your successes, life starts to lose its glitter, and when you don't understand that success is an ongoing process, a journey, then your achievements can feel like hollow victories.

Most people are now more likely to experience a fluctuating sense of success in their careers, and it is becoming harder to carve out a long-term future in one area as the pace of technological change is accelerating and driving change in the organisations in which we work and the businesses we start, and a plethora of new talent and competitors are always coming through.

Big versus small success

One of the traps of thinking about success is that we focus on a big goal, for example becoming the managing director of a company by the age of forty, or having a £5m business. This becomes the equivalent of having an ambition to climb Mount Everest, having a number-one hit, or playing professional football for your country.

You can only achieve big success like this by being successful over a series of small steps, over a period of time. Achieving big success is a journey. It requires lots of smaller successes and an understanding of the role of failure along the way.

Some people seem to sail effortlessly through life and achieve everything they want. The fact is, that during every journey, everyone will experience some aspect of failure. *It is how you respond to the failures you experience in life that determines how you will achieve your successes.*

At any one time there is only one person at the top of an organisation, there is only one person who is at the top of their sport, there is only one person or group at the top of the charts and there is only one winner of the Oscar for Best Actress in any one year.

This means that at any one time more people are experiencing relative failure than success. The point is, how do you classify your failures in your mind and what do you do with your successes?

James Dyson famously said: 'Enjoy failure and learn from it. You can never learn from success', and Thomas Edison, who patented the lightbulb, said: 'I haven't failed. I've just found 10,000 ways that won't work.'

Failures can be the springboards from which you learn how to be successful, or they can be the limiting judgements you accept about yourself as a person and your ability to achieve what you want in life. When you only focus on your big success and lose sight of the small successes and the value you get from the failures you experience along the way, you are creating a chasm in your mind that may seem unbridgeable.

The true value of failure

The best understanding of the value of failure comes from those who have experienced it and triumphed over it:

> 'Every adversity, every failure, every heartache carries with it the seed of an equal or greater benefit.'
>
> *Napoleon Hill*

> 'Only those who dare to fail greatly can ever achieve greatly.'
>
> *Robert F Kennedy*

> 'If you're not prepared to be wrong, you'll never come up with anything original.'
>
> *Ken Robinson*

> 'Success is not final, failure is not fatal: it is the courage to continue that counts.'
>
> *Winston Churchill*

> 'Failure is so important. We speak about success all the time. It is the ability to resist failure or use failure that often leads to greater success. I've met people who don't want to try for fear of failing.'
>
> *J K Rowling*

'Failures, repeated failures, are finger posts on the road to achievement. One fails forward toward success.'

C S Lewis

'Do not be embarrassed by your failures, learn from them and start again.'

Richard Branson

Exercise

Identify three times you have failed to achieve an objective you set yourself. (Important: this exercise is about developing the ability to look back and learn from mistakes, not rumination, which is the self-pitying state of ruing the luck you have had in life.)

Try and find failures that were really significant for you. (For example: a crucial exam, a business, your marriage, your relationship with your children.)

Now ask yourself the following questions:

• Do I take 100 per cent responsibility for my part in failure?

Until you take 100 per cent responsibility for your part in this failure, you will never look deep enough into the reasons for the failure and you won't be able to move forward to achieve the success you want. Do not be fooled by your brain's attempts to protect you from the emotional reactions you will experience as you do this exercise. Reactions such as: it was the wrong time, economic conditions were against me, or he/she didn't understand me. These are all examples of your brain trying to protect you from the pain of taking full responsibility for your part in this failure.

Remember Carl Jung's words: 'There is no coming to consciousness without pain.'

• What was my role in the failure I experienced?

This is the most crucial step in the process. In having the courage to be ruthlessly honest with yourself, you move from excuses to becoming empowered and taking responsibility for what happened. You can only move forward from an empowered state.

- With the benefit of hindsight, what could I have done differently to have prevented this failure?

Again your brain will try to protect you as you do this exercise. You may have an intuitive feeling of what was needed to be successful, but your brain may send you messages such as: 'I wouldn't have acted like that', 'I don't have that capability'.

These are just expressions of how disconnected you are from your natural resourcefulness and infinite potential.

- Taking what I have learnt about myself from the above questions, what situations am I currently facing that I could apply this learning to?

This is the step all truly successful people take. Some people do it instinctively, others are lucky enough to have mentors in their life who can help them see the learning and how to apply it.

It is this stage of the process that Henry Ford was referring to when he said: 'Thinking is the hardest work there is, which is probably the reason why so few engage in it.'

Your failures are training you

Celebrating your small successes will keep your motivation high and create the energy you will need to keep going towards your goal. The failures you experience are the equivalent of a psychological gym. They will help you become the person you need to be to deal with and hold on to success.

The paradox is that we love to watch this played out in the movies, films where the hero has to bounce back from failure to overcome his or her challenge and triumph in the end. The *Rocky* series comes to mind as the archetypal film of this genre but there are others which you might not think of as fulfilling this storyline: *Good Will Hunting, The Shawshank Redemption*, and even so called chick flicks such as *Erin Brockovich, Pretty Woman* and *Legally Blonde*. All of these films follow a pattern first described by Joseph Campbell, the hero's journey. This is examined in more detail in the chapter Understanding the Journey.

One of the myths of modern life is that as you become successful and earn more money, life becomes easier. It doesn't. It becomes more complex.

To maintain your success over time you have to become the person who can manage complexity in their life.

This is the personal growth journey.

In his book *Think and Grow Rich*, Napoleon Hill describes a moment at which successful people transcend the normal experiences of success and failure and can manifest success without struggle and when they want it. Let's call it the Napoleon Hill moment. It looks like this:

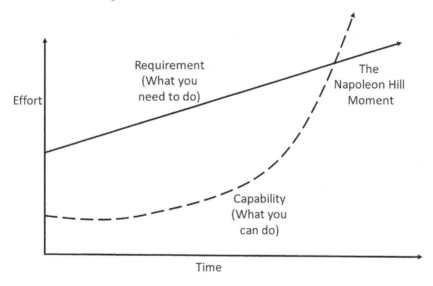

The straight line represents the journey of success, the gap between the curve and the straight line represents the failures we will experience on our journey, and the point where the lines cross represents the point at which we have learned how to create success effortlessly.

There is a saying:

Life doesn't give you what you want it gives you who you are.

To have success you have to become a person capable of bearing success. That is the personal growth journey we are all on.

Success lies elsewhere

One aspect of success that holds many people back from chasing and achieving their dream is the belief that success is the privilege of a few super-lucky, super-talented people.

The main reason for this is that we don't see the stresses and struggles they went through to achieve their success. This gives the impression that they are different to 'us'. That somehow they possess different skills and have found the magic formula. We look at successful people and say they were lucky to have been in the right place at the right time or to have the right idea at the right time.

Some people choose to hide their mistakes and disasters and others are prepared to be transparent. Richard Branson's biographies illustrate the risk, the uncertainty and the challenges that achieving big success brings in its wake.

Elton John in an interview on BBC radio talked of a musical he had written following his mega-successful collaboration with Tim Rice on *The Lion King*. He thought it was some of his best work and yet it was a commercial flop. Intuitively we know that chasing our dreams comes with a risk and there is the possibility of not being successful that goes along with it; so we hold back. Elton John didn't. If you are prepared to hold your dream in your conscious mind and go for it, it is always possible to achieve personal success and bring your dream to reality, as shown by Elton John and many others, even if it isn't commercially successful.

There is an added element required if you want to make money out of your dream. You have to create something that people want to buy. It is as simple as that.

When we look at people who have become successful in monetary terms there are two types:

- Those who have a simple idea that becomes bigger than they ever imagined, like The Beatles, J K Rowling, E L James and Terry Pratchett.
- Those who learn how to build businesses systematically and create ongoing long-term financial success. These include Warren Buffett, Richard Branson, Alan Sugar and Peter Jones.

Occasionally there are those who span both types and they can become super-wealthy. They include Steve Jobs, Bill Gates, Mark Zuckerberg and the Google guys.

Napoleon Hill describes 13 personal qualities possessed by all of the 500 very successful and wealthy people he interviewed for *Think and Grow Rich*. These included: the need for a deep yearning to succeed, positive self-talk, mastery of the subject, determination and intuition.

Published in 1937, Hill's book has become one of the staples of the personal development world and has been credited with the creation of more millionaires than any other guide.

Richard St John also interviewed 500 successful people to identify the characteristics that define them and in 2010, published his findings in *The 8 Traits that Successful People have in Common*.

He discovered that the people he interviewed all had incredible passion for what they did, worked incredibly hard at it, were totally focused on it, they pushed forward all the time, were always coming up with new ideas and wanting to improve what they did; and that overall they were driven to serve their clients or audience and they were willing to persevere to the end to achieve their goal.

If it is so simple, why is it that only a small proportion of people become successful and lead fulfilling lives?

You can't have everything

In the 1980s the freeing up of money, because of the changes that Margaret Thatcher's government had brought in to the UK's financial markets, made it much easier for the average person to get access to credit. Many people bought into the idea that anyone could become wealthy.

I didn't believe in that dream, even though I was actually living it. I had the big job, the big house, the beautiful wife and the lovely children.

I thought that my success came from the fortuitous coming together of being in the right place at the right time and happening to work with some people who believed in me and who hadn't seen through me – yet. So when I found myself in a bigger job that needed me to reproduce what I had achieved already, I didn't really know how to do it.

There are many examples of people who are living seemingly enchanted lives. On the face of it they have everything, but in reality they have lost one thing:

When you are successful you give up the ability to stay in the comfort zone of your smallness.

Marianne Williamson, the American spiritual teacher, captured this idea perfectly when she famously wrote that our greatest fear is that we are far more powerful than we realise.

It is only when we are prepared to give up our smallness and choose to make real the potential that lies within us that we can become truly successful.

Understanding Awareness

'*Two roads diverged in a yellow wood,*
And sorry I could not travel both

...

I took the one less traveled by,
And that has made all the difference.'

Robert Frost

The key to understanding your success is understanding awareness and how it impacts on the way you think.

The aspects of awareness that you must bring into your conscious thinking are:

- Awareness of your emotional state
- Awareness of your fears
- Awareness of your potential
- Awareness of your habits
- Awareness of compromise.

Awareness of your emotional state

The probability is that you have been driven by your emotional state for most of your life with little awareness of how it is affecting the way you see yourself or the way others perceive you.

Our emotions work at the most subtle of levels. The brain amplifies our emotions by secreting hormones, which is when we feel their physical effects: butterflies in the tummy, tense neck, fluttering heart, short and rapid breathing, and other physical effects of which you will not even be consciously aware. For example lowering of the immune system and digestive system and heightening of your internal alarm system. Your emotions are your brain's way of telling you to do something, to take action.

What we now know is that we are subconsciously sensitive to, and therefore aware of, the emotional state of the people in our environment. We can spot very slight changes in muscle tension in the face which may tell that there is some form of incongruity in the other person. We read this body language and try to interpret it. This then triggers the action of mirroring neurons in our brain that create a similar emotional state within us. This is the mechanism that makes emotions contagious.

It is imperative for anyone who is in a leadership position to be very aware of their emotional state and be able to manage it effectively. The consequences of not doing so will lead to a lack of internal coherence which will undermine the belief and determination needed for success to be realised; it will lead to a lack of resonance between you and the people you are trying to influence, and you will not be as effective in your communication.

It is difficult to build genuine and deep relationships when you are unaware of your emotional state and how it may be affecting other people because there are very few routes to success that will not require the help and support of other people.

Awareness of your fears

Fear is a silent killer. It kills dreams, ambition, self-belief and faith. But the biggest aspect of the silent nature of fear is that when we reach adulthood we are expected not to experience it.

Fear is an integral part of life. Understanding fear and learning how to live with it is a prerequisite of becoming successful and living to your full potential. Jack Canfield, author of *Chicken Soup for the Soul*, had a wonderful saying about it: 'Everything you want is on the other side of fear.'

So why is it that some people seem to laugh in the face of fear and others crumble in its glare?

The paradox of age is that the things that frighten us as children we tend to grow out of, and what held no fear for us then can become blockages in our minds.

The key to dealing with fear is to remember that it is a natural concoction of the mind and its objective is to keep you safe.

Fear is one of the primal emotions. It is generated in the most primitive parts of the brain, the reptilian and limbic systems, and it has the most power over your thinking. Fear is the mind's natural way of telling you that you are moving into the unknown and that danger might be lurking there. It can affect your decision-making at the most minute level and can be at the root of major disagreements with your loved ones, friends and work colleagues.

Recently I asked a client how she had enjoyed her skiing holiday. She had enjoyed it, but the most memorable moment had been when her husband had suggested she take the black run from the top of the mountain back to the ski lodge. My friend is an experienced skier but she felt this run was too much for her and she refused to go. Her friends gently mocked her and so she relented and started off down the slope. After a few seconds she tumbled and slid down the slope on her back, losing her skis and poles along the way. Luckily she wasn't hurt.

When she finally returned to the ski lodge she didn't lose her temper with her husband in front of their skiing friends (we'd been working together for a few months to help her develop her emotional intelligence). This was the part of the story that she was most proud of and which she wanted to tell me about. As we talked more about this experience she admitted that she probably had enough skill to ski the run but that it was her fear that had prevented her from 'leaning in' and going for it.

The fears

As you look at the list that follows you might immediately think of people who exhibit exactly the opposite trait to the fear described. Do not worry about this. The list of fears does not imply that everyone experiences them, that you should experience them or that if you don't experience them you are in some way not normal.

It's just a list to help you raise your awareness of them and therefore be in a position to manage your reactions appropriately should you experience them.

Ancient Chinese philosopher Lao Tzu said: 'If you realise that all things change, there is nothing you will try to hold on to. If you are not afraid of dying, there is nothing you cannot achieve.'

Death also describes the coming to an end of something. In brackets you will see each fear described in terms of the death it represents. This will give you another way of thinking about fear and hopefully another way of overcoming it.

The fear of being becoming corrupt (the death of integrity)

Most people have an innate sense of right and wrong, but we frequently face situations where the decisions we have to make do not have clear-cut outcomes and we worry about making the right decision for the right reasons. Some people are just corrupt and all societies have created laws to deal with these types of people. This fear can create internal angst as we wrestle with our consciences about the choices we have to make. Not overcoming this fear will lead to procrastination and inaction.

The fear of being unloved and unlovable (the death of love)

Being loved is a core human need (see page 86). It exists within all of us and drives all sorts of behaviours. The fear of being unloved and/or unlovable can drive behaviours such as subservience and self-denial as sufferers will do what they need to gain favour and love from the people in their life. This fear can also drive the exact opposite behaviours. After all, if you feel unloved or unlovable what's the point of trying to be loved?

The fear of being unworthy (the death of esteem)

This fear will stop you from seeing the value that you bring to the world and from appreciating your successes. You may even reject the recognition that other people give you. This will undermine your relationships, both personal and professional. It can be seen in workaholics and perfectionists where nothing they create is ever good enough.

The fear of lacking a unique identity (the death of self)

We are born unique and our life experiences ensure that we all have a unique perspective of the world. People who experience this fear cannot see their uniqueness in the world. This can result in workaholicism in an attempt to become indispensable in your role, and it can lead to a fear of mainstream culture, which would not differentiate you from everybody else. It can lead to resistance to change and rigidity as a means of hanging on to your identity.

The fear of being inadequate (the death of ability)

People living with this fear feel that they have to be experts at everything. In any topic of conversation they will know more than you or at least claim to. This person will also have done more than you and experienced everything in more extreme circumstances than you. This fear is generated by the fact that there is more knowledge available than is knowable. It is the fear of the person who has a fixed mindset, and while it might lead them to know a lot of facts, it can make it difficult for them to show their vulnerability. This fear can also show up as an obsession with health in an attempt to avoid the feeling of helplessness that can accompany ill-health.

The fear of being without support (the death of community)

People with this fear worry about becoming disconnected from others and out of harmony with the world around them. They will do anything to avoid conflict so that they can be part of a harmonious group. This is the fear of being unable to survive and thrive by your own efforts. In its extreme it leads to the inability to make any decisions and indicates a lack of self-belief and confidence. This can also cause inaction and procrastination because of the potential for criticism and the perceived loss of support that comes with it. It manifests itself in the fear of being rejected. This can become a major block for those who live in tight-knit communities and also for people who do not like selling.

The fear of failure (the death of achievement)

The fear of failure is the main reason why most people do not try and achieve their dreams. It can manifest as a complete lack of ambition or in excessive drive, or unusual levels of motivation. People who experience super-motivation can become disappointed by the people in their life whose ambitions do not match theirs. Those who deny their own ambitions may blame their circumstances for their own lack of success rather than look inwards at the fear of failing that is holding them back.

The fear of success (the death of innocence)

This fear is rooted in an innate understanding that success will change us and our most important relationships. It also has roots in our beliefs about money. Most religions condemn the accumulation of monetary wealth and this is programmed into us through sayings such as '*It is easier for a camel to pass through the eye of a needle than a rich man to get into heaven*'.

With such programming from an early age it can be difficult as an adult to move past the psychological barriers created in childhood. It creates an unconscious association that rich people are inherently bad and therefore we can unconsciously become money and success averse.

The fear of being controlled by others (the death of power)

Deepak Chopra said that the universe works through dynamic exchange. The fear of being controlled by others comes from a lack of understanding that we should give what we seek, and a lack of understanding about the power of showing vulnerability. People with this fear can become unyielding as their overriding need is to be seen as strong and independent. Negotiating and compromise are difficult for them.

The fear of poverty (the death of safety and security)

This is very often the main driver of very rich people and can stop those who have accumulated vast fortunes from actually enjoying the advantages that their wealth brings. It is a strong motivating force but can lead to a risk-averse approach to life.

The fear of old age (the death of opportunity)

This comes when a life has not been lived with any sense of purpose or meaning. People who believe they have led full and meaningful lives rarely have this fear. This is about looking back on life. In the book *The*

Top Five Regrets of the Dying: A Life Transformed by the Dearly Departing, Bronnie Ware lists the main regrets of patients she tended as a nurse in their last days. The biggest regret was that of not having the courage to have lived a life true to themselves rather than living the life expected of them by others.

I was to witness this personally as I watched my father decline in the years after his early retirement due to ill health. As a young man he had wanted to be a doctor but had bowed to his parent's wishes to become an accountant. Whilst he was undoubtedly talented in this area and successful, it was his words on his retirement that will stay with me for ever: 'Thank God I don't have to do that anymore.'

He was only fifty-three when he uttered those words and his remaining years could have seen him embracing the opportunities of this new period in his life. Instead I watched a man crippled by the fears of his frailties start to lead a smaller and smaller life as he gave into the fear.

A recent piece of commercial research by the company CloudBuy, featured by the *Daily Telegraph,* suggests that the fear of old age hits many people as early as fifty and the top concerns are: health issues, failing mind and loss of independence.

Exercise: how to deal with your fears

- Do you have any fears that regularly play on your mind? If so, list them. Bringing them into the open has the effect of reducing their power.
- Admit that you are experiencing fear and consider whether it is legitimate in each case. Talk about them with someone who knows you. This may be uncomfortable but a different perspective will help you to deal with them.
- Take considered action. Fears exist in our minds, when we take action to confront them we provide data to our mind to show that we can overcome the fear. You will discover that you are more than capable of dealing with the thing you were frightened of.

But: Seek professional help if your fears have developed to the point where they are debilitating.

Awareness of your potential

Your potential is just that – potential. It is the potential to do and achieve something tomorrow that you haven't done or achieved so far in your life.

Your potential is only ever reached when you put a mental cap on it. There are two dimensions to the capping of your potential: your beliefs and the people in your life.

Your beliefs

There is a way of thinking, certainly in Western societies, that the older you get the less you are able to do. Of course there is an element of truth to this when it comes to the physical aspect of life, but age is only a cap on your potential if you choose it to be. Your potential reveals itself to you in different ways at different stages of your life and at different steps on your journey, but only if you are open to seeing it and accepting it.

The key to your potential lies in maintaining your curiosity towards life.

T S Elliot knew this: 'I don't believe one grows older. I think that what happens early on in life is that at a certain age one stands still and stagnates.'

The only time you become disconnected from your potential is the moment you decide to stop learning.

The people in your life

If you are very lucky you will have someone in your life who will help you to bring out your potential. These people are sometimes referred to as mentors. If you do not have anyone in your life who can help you fulfil your potential there is now an industry of professional coaches to turn to.

All through life you will meet people who will tell you what you can't do. To see and achieve your own potential can sometimes require you to leave behind those who would prefer you to keep your mind closed to your potential. Maybe your ambition highlights the paucity in their lives. If so, run as fast as you can from their influence. Some people will seek to hold you back because of the unresolved fears in their lives. If you have the strength you can help them to overcome their fears so they can support you as you step out on your journey.

As I mentioned my father experienced this through his childhood as his parents demanded that he give up his interest in medicine to become an accountant because their belief was that the world of accountancy was a more secure way to earn a safe living. Whilst my father was successful in this line of work it left him feeling unfulfilled and dissatisfied with his life.

Many children experience this pressure from their parents; because the parent does not understand the child's world they are fearful of it and try to pressure their children to follow a path they understand and are comfortable with.

Your potential is the expression of your possibility rather than your actuality and there is only one way to activate it.

Ultimately you have to have faith in yourself and you have to develop a growth mindset. Audrey Hepburn said it best: 'Nothing is impossible, the word itself says I'm possible!'

Awareness of your habits

In our habits lies the picture we give to the world of who we are.

We can develop habits in every aspect of our lives: from the way we breathe, to the way we eat, to the way we walk, to the way we react to situations, even how we greet our friends.

The brain has evolved to do things in the most efficient way possible, meaning it develops patterns of behaviour that it doesn't have to put energy into thinking about. We have millions of habits programmed into us, happening subconsciously. You might say that the way the heart beats and the way we breathe are controlled by the brain at a subconscious level, but we can develop habits even in relation to these core bodily functions. We can become addicted (a habit taken to its extreme) to our heart being in an excited state and pumping fast and hard. We can develop patterns in our breathing where the habit becomes one of short, shallow breaths rather than the longer, fuller deep breaths that represent the body's natural rhythm.

Earlier I mentioned Daniel Kahneman's idea that the brain has two systems, fast and slow. Fast makes quick judgments, slow requires intense focus and operates methodically. These two systems interact continually, using what he calls the heuristic process.

For example:

You come home from work one day to find your partner in a furious mood. You ask what's the matter and they say 'nothing'. It's so obviously not the truth that your brain is now working at full speed trying to work out why your partner is so angry.

Was it something you did? Was it something you said? Was it something that happened at their work? Is it to do with the kids?

Your brain is whirring so fast that you can't keep track of the thoughts you are experiencing.

What your brain is doing, using the fast system, is trying to match patterns of behaviours it is familiar with, to make sense of the situation it has just encountered. Your brain is jumping to the next most likely reason that would help explain the mood of your partner. The fast system works by comparing experiences that already exist in your memory. It can't bring new factors into the equation. That can only be done through system two, the slow, conscious-thinking aspect of the brain.

The brain has evolved to assess situations as fast as possible and store the experiences as a memory so that they are readily available for the fast part of the brain to use. This is the underlying process by which our habits get formed.

Going back to your partner, who you've come home to find in a bad mood... if this is a regular occurrence then it is likely that you will have developed a habitual response to it. Depending on how well you know your partner you might leave them alone to work things out in their own mind, or get them to talk with you, or offer them a drink.

In all cases you have not engaged the slow, thinking brain. It is your fast brain that has caused you to behave in this instinctive manner. Becoming aware of your habitual behaviours is a vital step in freeing your potential.

Do you habitually see the opportunity or the downside of every situation?

When your reactions to the world become habitual you take away your ability to choose, and as Viktor Frankl noted: 'Freedom lies in our ability to choose our response to any situation.'

There is now research to suggest that physical addictions to recreational drugs, excessive drinking or smoking are the brain's response to dealing with situations that it finds difficult or even impossible to deal with.

You do not have to be a prisoner of your habits. If you are not achieving what you want in your life or you have now decided that you have something specific and important that you want to achieve, the removal of old habits that are not serving you and the creation of new habits that will is the essential first step. But it is the step that most people are unwilling to take.

Einstein is reputed to have said that the definition of insanity is doing the same things but expecting different results, and yet this is what most people do. You can recognise this by the way people bemoan their luck or the state of the economy or their horrible boss or their wife or husband or their children. They are happy to blame every circumstance without factoring in their habitual choices and behaviours.

Becoming aware of your habits and developing habits that serve you as you look to fulfil your potential is vital for bringing success into your life.

Awareness of compromise

Compromise is one of the hidden landmines that will derail you on your journey. Compromise is misunderstood by most of us. It has evolved as a process to resolve disputes, but the problem with compromise is that we do not look at the underlying reasons for the dispute but at the dispute itself.

When you start to think of the nature of compromise you may feel the pressure to give up your dreams to satisfy the needs of someone else. But the act of compromise sits in one place only, inside of you. Beware of the person that asks you to compromise your desires and needs so that they can fulfil theirs, because this is the way compromise usually works in our society. It should serve all parties involved, but it rarely does.

Compromise always leads to dissatisfaction because, in the end, the person you are compromising with is yourself.

Disputes occur at the following levels:

- Within yourself: we are often in dispute with ourselves, drawn into quandaries about how to spend our time and resources between our work, our partner, our children, our family and our friends and hobbies. You may have additional caring commitments on top. As there are only twenty-four hours in a day there are only so many hours we can give to each aspect of our lives. For most people the need to earn money takes priority, but it is the way that people use the remainder of their time that can cause conflict. When you feel inner conflict it makes decision-making more difficult and success less likely.

- With someone you are close to: think of someone close to you, with whom you have an ongoing deep relationship. Ask yourself: What percentage of the relationship am I responsible for? You will probably have answered 50 per cent. But there's an inherent problem with this approach. By definition it must mean you think that the other person in this relationship is also responsible for 50 per cent. But where does your 50 per cent finish and the other person's start? And if something goes wrong in the relationship, from which 50 per cent did it go wrong? When you are only prepared to take 50 per cent responsibility for a relationship, you are immediately on the path to compromise. This principle applies in every relationship and every plan you have and there is only one solution. You have to have a very clear vision of how you want the relationship or the plan to be and you have to take 100 per cent responsibility for the nurturing and maintenance of the vision. When you abdicate even 10 per cent of the responsibility to someone else you have already compromised. If you are now asking: but how do I take 100 per cent responsibility in a two-person relationship? The answer is by giving everything you can give to the relationship, unconditionally. This means accepting that you cannot make the other person do what they do not want to do.

When you can achieve this level of thinking then you will truly be living life on your terms, and the people in your life will also be experiencing a new level of freedom, respect and compassion.

I was lucky enough to have come across the idea of unconditional giving soon after I left the marital home, through my reading. I was petrified of losing my kids. I was aware of too many dads whose relationship with their kids dies after separation from the mother. And I resolved that would not happen to me. So I called my children every night when they got back from school to let them know I was still there. Most times they didn't want to talk to me and had nothing to say. I would see them on a Friday night or Sunday lunchtime and that would be my one time with them. I learned very quickly that any emotional connection I asked for would be resisted. This could be very hurtful in the moment as my fear of being rejected by my own kids surfaced from within. It was my reading about unconditional giving that helped me to recognise when I was putting my needs ahead of theirs. As I found a way to let go of my need to have my love reciprocated on a like-for-like-basis they slowly came to feel that they had the freedom to show me their love in their own way.

I now have a wonderful relationship with both of my children and I firmly believe that it is a result of my learning how to give unconditionally.

Awareness of your level of awareness

Awareness exists at many different levels, from the basic instinct of primitive lifeforms to the complex thoughts and ideas that we are able to create and hold in our human minds. Some people still only have awareness at a very low, almost animalistic level and they live purely by their instincts at the level of emotional reaction. Others have developed higher levels of awareness and through this have developed their ability to choose their response to life.

Remember, our freedom lies in our ability to choose our response.

If you are operating at a lower level your choices are made for you, driven by your hormones and the unconscious thoughts of your mind.

When you have developed awareness you have the ability to choose and with this awareness you create options and opportunities that people who are less aware cannot see.

The communication between people of higher and lower levels of awareness is difficult because they are looking at different worlds. It is as if one is thriving in the rich jungle of life and the other is existing in a desert. One cannot conceive of the other's circumstances.

When you reach a higher level of awareness there can be a temptation to try and help those at a lower level to come up to your level, but it is an impossible task. Lao Tzu said: 'When the student is ready the teacher will come.' This is as true today as it was 2,500 years ago. For the student who isn't ready the teacher will never come, because the student cannot see her yet.

Success is not the child of intelligence. If so the professors and PhDs of the world would be the richest people on the planet and the truth is that many of them are very poor.

Success is the child of your level of awareness; when you can accept this principle and you learn the way to develop your awareness, you are on the way to true success and you are most definitely on the road less travelled.

RESOURCEFULNESS

'Intellectual growth should commence at birth and cease only at death.'
Albert Einstein

I had most definitely reached my dark night of the soul.

Sitting on the floor of my apartment, glass of red wine in one hand and the bottle in the other, I contemplated the ruins of my marriage and my corporate career and the fearful uncertainty of what lay ahead for me.

I had reached that place where the pain of staying the same was greater than the pain of change. I was opening myself up to the possibility that perhaps I didn't know everything. As someone who had always regarded himself as fiercely independent and capable of working things out, it was a huge step forward. I was thinking of another of Albert Einstein's insights into the working of the mind: 'It is only when we accept our limitations that we move beyond them.'

During my long dark night I had finally accepted that I was indeed like my father. I realised that it was my resistance to the idea of being like my father and not the fact that I was like him that had been the root cause of my difficulties. Having become open to the idea of seeking help, I went on a search for information.

It's amazing what you can see when your eyes are open. Suddenly it was wherever I looked: counsellors, therapists, coaches, self-help books, personal development programmes going back a hundred years. I started to notice two trends in the books I was reading: the tendency of many authors to end up on a path of religion, and particularly Christianity, as an expression of their spirituality, and secondly, this perennial idea that the answer lies within you.

My frustration came from the fact that the books I was reading were very happy to present the statement to me but they seemed very unwilling to try and answer the question that follows on: If the answer lies within me, what is it that I've got that is the answer?

While I was sitting in pieces on my living-room floor, I certainly didn't feel that the answer lay within me; far from it. All I could think of was that what was inside of me had got me to the state I was in. The self-help programmes I was reading about were trying to get me to see a better future for myself by setting goals and visualising an abundant destination, but from where I was lying that felt about as likely as a two-week package trip to the moon.

Resourceful versus unresourceful states

NLP (neuro-linguistic programming), created in the 1970s, embodies the idea that we move in and out of resourceful and unresourceful states. The notion is that we already have all the resources we need to succeed, but sometimes our state of mind prevents these resources from being readily available to us.

There are no unresourceful people, only unresourceful states. People already have the resources they need to succeed. Sometimes they get themselves into a state of mind (overwhelm, sadness, anger) that prevents these resources from being readily available.

As I thought about the idea of 'no unresourceful people', a new notion was starting to form. Its basis came from reading about how babies learn. Babies don't have to be taught to learn; they have an inbuilt instinct for learning, as their brains develop. Assuming no physical impairments, what they learn and how fast they learn is dependent on their environment, predominantly their parents, in those very early days, months and years.

In their early years of play, children imagine themselves in all kinds of roles and ask innocent questions without concern that they might appear stupid, but it is not too long before they become self-conscious.

The transition from this age of innocence to self-consciousness may mark the point at which we start to lose our access to the infinite potential of our resourcefulness. Boundaries are placed on our resourcefulness, which becomes limited by the feedback of incentives and punishments we receive throughout our infant, child and teenage years. You might remember times when you were told to stop asking questions or were told off for playing with fire. Through this process, by the time we reach early adulthood our willingness to ask questions and play, which came from our innocence, has largely gone. This is replaced by a framework of boundaries, within which we expect to receive approval from the people whose patronage we need for our advancement in society. We start to rely on behaviours and patterns of thinking that are effective in getting us what we want, but which represent just a small proportion of the potential that we have available to us.

These become our noticeable traits and they are what people both recognise and judge us by.

Perhaps you have tried to explain to someone that you have the potential to do a particular job, and they have looked at you blankly. There is often a gap between the potential we feel within ourselves and the potential that other people can see in us. Sometimes people can see potential in us that we ourselves can't see. Sometimes we see potential in ourselves that others can't see. Once I was refused a job based on my score from a standard personality test. I knew it was a job I could easily have done and been good at because I had been successful in a similar role, but because my profile didn't match the specified profile I was turned down.

Some weeks later I had the exact opposite experience, again from a prospective employer using the same personality profile. This time my profile was just what they were looking for and I got the job. At one level I was happy but I still didn't think it was right that a judgement about my potential had been made as a result of someone's interpretation of my questionnaire.

We make judgements about others' potential all the time and very often based on evidence that has no relevance.

Strengths and talents

The strengths movement is based on the principle that it is more efficient for us to concentrate and work on developing our strengths than it is to work on overcoming our weaknesses.

Marcus Buckingham, author of *Go Put Your Strengths to Work*, and Tom Rath, author of *StrengthsFinder*, are both good reads in this area. For those who can identify their strengths early on in life, and more importantly, enjoy what they are good at, this is a very good strategy for success. But your strength might not be something you enjoy or want to spend your time on. For example, I am good at maths, so when I was at school I was guided towards accountancy and banking for my career path. But these are not my thing. I can do accounts but they don't make my heart sing. A strength is something you are good at but a strengthener is something that makes you feel good when you are doing it.

Plus, life has a tendency to throw problems our way that don't fit nicely into our areas of strength and we still have to deal those problems.

Exercise: strengths versus strengtheners

If you want to understand the difference between strengths and strengtheners this very simple exercise will help you.

1. List what you're not very good at and when you do them they drain your energy or make you feel crabby. These are your weaknesses and weakeners.
2. List what you're good at but which you don't really like doing that much. These are your strengths but are weakeners.
3. List what you're not very good at but you like doing and they make you feel good. These are your weak strengtheners.
4. List what you're good at and that you like doing and make you feel energised when you are doing them. These are your strong strengtheners.

Life never gives you the opportunity to *only* do what you love doing. Most people I meet have put little conscious time into considering their strengtheners and weakeners because there is a tendency for most of us to think in terms of putting up with the things we don't enjoy in our lives. The trouble with this approach is that we end up bemoaning the little amount of time we get to do what we really love.

Either delegate the jobs you don't enjoy or reframe the way you look at a problem. For example, let's say you have to write the boss's monthly report. If you could change the way you look at the monthly report from a senseless waste of your time to an opportunity for you to see the big picture in your company, it will help you to produce the report without expending as much emotional energy in resistance.

If you enjoy an activity but you are not very good at, is it worth the investment to become better? We tend to enjoy doing the things we're good at, so with some training and development these activities could become strong strengtheners.

Talent versus resourcefulness

Calvin Coolidge was the thirtieth president of the United States, serving from 1923 to 1929. He flagged up the fundamental difference between talent and resourcefulness in the following paragraph:

'Nothing in this world can take the place of persistence. Talent will not: nothing is more common than unsuccessful men with talent. Genius will not: unrewarded genius is almost a proverb. Education will not: the world is full of educated derelicts. Persistence and determination alone are omnipotent.'

Persistence and determination are aspects of resourcefulness, not talent.

The author Stephen King perhaps captured it a little more succinctly: 'Talent is cheaper than table salt. What separates the talented individual from the successful one is a lot of hard work.'

When I was at school I knew a big strong lad who was a very good sportsman. Great at football, a top runner and athlete, but these were not areas he wanted to put any time into. Girls, drinking and smoking all came higher up his list of priorities. Not surprisingly, as we progressed through school he slipped out of the football team, he was no longer the fastest runner or the longest shot putter and his inherent talents ended up counting for nothing. I don't know what happened to him but I can remember feeling sad that he couldn't see his own potential and allowed it to waste away.

People who use their resourcefulness can outshine those with more natural talents.

In sport those who rise to the very top of their game are usually noted for their dedication and willingness to work hard to develop and make the most of their talent.

The retired golfer Gary Player became one of the most successful players in the history of the game. He was never regarded as one of the games naturals but won the hearts of fans around the world with his fighting spirit and his now famous motto: 'The more I practise the luckier I seem to get.'

It is no coincidence that the Paralympic Games has become such a draw for spectators. The resourcefulness required to overcome disabilities and perform at such levels makes for emotional viewing and admiration for the athletes.

You may not have heard of Tony Pidgley, who started life as an orphan in a Barnardo's home and went on to create one of the largest British house-building companies, Berkeley Group Holdings, becoming a multi-millionaire.

These people are all examples of the power of resourcefulness. Ultimately it is our resourcefulness that takes us to where we want to go, not our talent.

What should I spend my time on?

Can we change our behaviours? The answer to this question has to be: yes – but only if you want to.

If this wasn't true, there would be no such thing as personal growth. We only become what we are capable of being through our ability to learn and adapt our behaviours according to our experiences.

You can see by observing your friends and people you've known for decades that behaviour does change over time. Or you can see it in public figures such as Richard Branson and David Beckham, whose public persona has changed since the early years of their careers.

So the question is not 'Can a leopard change his spots?' but 'Are you aware of how your behaviours are changing?'

In 2000, three researchers from Harvard University, Marinova-Todd, Marshall and Snow, studied the ability of children versus adults to learn a second language. Very interestingly, they found that it was motivation, and not age, that was the critical factor in learning the new language. This goes contrary to received wisdom about the effect of age on our brains.

Is the idea of resourcefulness gripping you yet?

What if we are born with infinite potential, and the degree to which we realise that potential is dependent on the life experiences we have? If this was true, then we could truly claim that 'the answer lies within us'; in our ability to feel our resourcefulness, have faith in it and give it the opportunity to flourish.

The important factor is not what anyone else thinks about your resourcefulness but what you think about it. In order to realise your potential, you need to believe in your resourcefulness and the natural tendency of resourcefulness to grow as we experience success.

What are the potential traits that we carry inside us?

In 1936, the psychologist Gordon Allport published his lexicon of personality traits. He scoured different cultures and languages to try and identify every word used to describe a form of human behaviour. The list runs to about 4,000 words, many of them so obscure as to be useless today (I suspect they weren't in common usage when Allport compiled his list). For example, antrorse, bathycolpian and hebetudinous are not words I have come across outside of his lexicon. His work illustrates just how difficult it is to capture the full breadth and depth of the human personality. Why else would we need so many words to capture the essence of what it is to be human?

But just because someone has gone out of their way to list all of the words that could possibly describe a human quality doesn't mean that we possess all those qualities. The question is, did we possess the potential when we were born and if we did, what happened to that potential as we grew up?

The key to understanding your resourcefulness and your hidden potential lies in separating the idea of your resourcefulness, or your personal qualities, from your talent. Here are some examples to illustrate the difference:

Talents	Resourcefulness
Playing a sport	Determination
Managing a business	Persistence
Acting	Compassion
Playing a musical instrument	Empathy
Writing a computer programme	Desire
Writing a novel	Flexibility
Speaking a second language	Spontaneity
Running a marathon	Versatility
Training dogs	Courage
Painting a picture	Faith
Photography	Discernment

In all cases talent has to be developed and applied with discipline (a resource) for it to serve us effectively.

Accessing your resourcefulness

When we experience grief, anger and fear, our behaviours are driven at the primal level of these core emotions. Think of when you last felt high emotion and try and remember your ability to think clearly and effectively in those times.

Primal emotions evolved to keep us physically safe, but they can cut off our ability to access our thinking brain so we become less resourceful. Therefore, we might assume that our ability to remain in a resourceful state is directly related to our perception of the level of threat or risk in which we find ourselves. Taken to its extreme is a state referred to as 'negative panic' when people become immobilised with fear.

One of the few recorded examples of this was captured in a newspaper report in 1963 from the *Wilmington Post* in the US. It reported the deaths of a number of people in a plane crash who were found still strapped to their seats even though they had time to release their seat belts and escape through the emergency doors. Apparently they had been waiting for instructions from the flight attendant. They were rendered totally unresourceful because of their predicament.

The opposite is also true. We see examples every day of people who become more resourceful in the face of threat and risk. This includes selfless bravery at accident and disaster scenes and those who thrive in high-risk situations, from poker players to downhill skiers and deep-sea divers to entrepreneurs. These people have learned how to access their inner resourcefulness under pressure.

Accessing your resourcefulness is a choice, but like all muscles that are not exercised, it will get weaker over time.

For example, you see this in people who:

- have failed to exercise their mental flexibility, who become set in their ways
- have been beaten down by life to such a degree that they lose all determination and perseverance
- have lost the ability to show kindness and compassion
- have lost their sense of judgement and do ill-considered things in the heat of the moment
- have become so narrow-minded that they cannot tolerate anyone with a different point of view.

The potential of your resourcefulness is always with you and you can reactivate it at any time if you have the will.

The way that we are educated by our parents and teachers has immense impact on the self-image we create for ourselves, and this is pivotal in influencing whether we develop a fixed or growth mindset.

As we grow up we form beliefs about our capabilities and our areas of natural talent. We also construct a belief about our ability to develop and grow. If we think we can learn and develop, we do, and if we don't think we can grow and develop, we don't. I have seen this many times with people I have worked with. It happens with young people who have been told that they are no good and they then go on to believe this through their life, and it can happen in adulthood when our potential to develop at work is supported or thwarted. As Albert Einstein famously said: 'All that is valuable in human society depends upon the opportunity for development accorded the individual.'

Some people have the natural inner drive to overcome the judgements and actions of people who have hindered their natural motivation to learn and grow, but many others do not.

Your attitude towards learning and growth are fundamental to your self-perception and the inherent resourcefulness you feel within. Remember that your resourcefulness is not the same as your talent: you use your resourcefulness to enable you to develop your talent to its potential.

Classification of core personal qualities

In my book *ResourcefulMe* I propose the idea that we all have 31 core qualities and these then sub-divide into a further 150 qualities that we can bring to bear whenever the need demands.

You might wonder why it is necessary to list and describe these qualities, thinking that surely it is a 'given' or just common sense that we possess them. However, my experience is far from that. It is a lack of belief in these basic qualities that causes many people to hold off from pursuing their dreams or confronting their demons.

For ease, just the core qualities are listed here.

Adaptability: The ability to cope with changing circumstances efficiently, effectively and in an appropriate time scale. Our ability to deal with the pace of change of life is key to living a useful, meaningful and productive life. It also evokes the qualities of flexibility, versatility and compliance.

Alertness: The facility to be conscious of what is going on around you. It also evokes the qualities of observation, concentration, attentiveness, consideration, sensitivity, understanding, awareness and courtesy.

Ambition: A strong feeling of wanting to be successful in life and achieve great things. It also evokes the qualities of desire, drive and mastery

Analytical: The ability to separate things, situations or processes into their constituent elements in order to study or examine them, draw conclusions, or solve problems. This also evokes the qualities of being cerebral, critical thinking, questioning, strategic thinking, problem solving and being studious.

Assurance: To have confidence in one's personal ability and/or status. It also evokes the qualities of decisiveness, modesty and humility.

Broadmindedness: The willingness to assimilate and tolerate a wide range of ideas and behaviour. It also the evokes qualities of being non-judgmental, tolerance, acceptance of criticism, acceptance of rejection, the ability to learn, the willingness to ask for help, curiosity and inquisitiveness.

Commitment: The devotion or dedication to a cause, person or relationship. It has the implication of duration and time in relation to the task at hand or the cause. It also evokes the qualities of consistency, of being unwavering, loyalty and dedication.

Communication: In its basic form communication is the exchange of information between people, but to be effective it has to become the achievement of shared meaning. It also evokes these qualities: advocacy, persuasion, the ability to explain, negotiation, listening and performing.

Composure: The quality of a calm or tranquil state of mind, frequently recognised by its absence as much as its presence.

Conscientiousness: Being hard working and showing great care. It evokes the qualities of accuracy, attention to detail and diligence.

Courage: The ability to face danger, fear, difficulty, uncertainty, or pain without being overcome by fear or being deflected from a chosen course of action. It evokes the qualities of being enterprising, being innovative and the ability to hold one's nerve.

Dependability. This is the quality which allows trust to develop. It evokes the qualities of being punctual and reliable.

Determination: Is the firmness of intention to reach a goal or achieve an objective irrespective of any obstacles which might get in the way. It evokes the qualities of: perseverance, resolve and resilience.

Emotional Maturity: Understanding your emotions and the effect they have on you and the people around you. It evokes the qualities of empathy, patience, self-management.

Generosity: The willingness to give your resources freely to the benefit of somebody or something without the need for receiving anything in return. This can be expressed in material ways and spiritually. It also evokes the qualities of kindness and being loving.

Honesty: The quality of being truthful. It is also the qualities of sincerity, integrity and openness.

Imagination: Being good at thinking of new ideas or at visualising things that have never been seen or experienced before. It evokes the qualities of being visionary, creativity, conceptualisation and the ability to connect ideas.

Industry: The quality of being hard-working and busy in a directed way that produces results. It evokes the qualities of being productive and effort.

Inwardness: The ability to connect with the beliefs and values that make up the inner you and that drive your actions. It evokes the qualities of being principled, conviction and faith.

Judgement: The ability to evaluate and balance many factors before making a decision or taking a course of action. It evokes the qualities of perspective, realism, a sense of history and ancestry, appreciation, gratitude, celebration, caution, care, prudence, risk management, discretion, vigilance, being discriminating, being ethical, discernment and the appreciation of beauty.

Justice: The quality of demonstrating fairness and reasonableness in the way people are treated and decisions are made. Fairness – the quality of remaining impartial. Being reasonable – the quality of not expecting or demanding more than is possible or achievable.

Manager: The ability to organise and make things happen in an orderly manner.

Memory: The ability to recall facts at the relevant moments. A fundamental resource that requires development.

Nurturing: The quality of giving tender care, protection and encouragement to help someone or something grow and develop. It evokes the quality of trust.

Optimism: The tendency to take a hopeful and positive view of the future in a way that is inspiring to yourself and those around you. It evokes the qualities of motivation, enthusiasm, being energetic and stamina.

People Oriented: Being inclined to seek out and enjoy the company of other people and to have that reciprocated. It evokes the qualities of being amiable, friendly, networking, being a team player, cooperation and being inclusive.

Resourcefulness: The degree to which you can access the full range of the infinite potential that exists within you. It evokes the qualities of ingenuity, initiative, independence and quick thinking.

Responsible: The ability to hold yourself accountable for an action or result of an action and to identify the next course of action required in order to achieve an objective. It evokes the qualities of leadership, self-discipline, time-management and ownership.

Self-Awareness: The ability to be aware of the influences on your mind and the consequences these have on your thinking and the way you behave. It evokes the qualities of assertiveness, personal development, direction and purpose.

Spontaneity: The ability to act in the moment.

Will: The conscious control of your mind and thinking towards a desired objective.

Disclaimer:
I do not claim that this list is the complete description of every possible state of resourcefulness it is possible to display. However, after extensive research I believe it covers the spectrum of personal qualities without leaving any big gaps and that by considering these aspects of resourcefulness you can usefully reflect on your ability to access these qualities in the moment you need them.

Activating your Resourcefulness

Activating your resourcefulness is a two-step process. The first is an act of faith and requires you to accept that you have inside you the potential of

ALL of the qualities that have been listed. Over the years you will have developed some of these qualities, allowed others to wither and disappear from your repertoire, and others you are likely to have been told you don't possess.

You will notice that the list of attributes that comprise your resourcefulness does not include any reference to talents; for example, the ability to run, or sing, or act, or draw, or kick a football or hit a golf ball, or do maths or write prose.

How can I find out what my talents are?

Some people are multi-talented, and others are gifted in a single area. Most of us travel through life never identifying or developing our talents to their potential. Developing your talents to the level of mastery requires commitment and single-mindedness, which can be difficult if you have a busy family life or demanding career. This dilemma has always been part of human existence and is part of the journey that we all experience.

Understanding the difference between your resourcefulness, your personal qualities, and your talent is a key step on the road to personal development.

In 2001, during England's last game in their World Cup qualifier, trailing two goals to one against Greece, 2½ minutes into injury time, David Beckham hit the most sublime free kick of his career. It looped and curled over the defensive wall of players out of the reach of the goal keeper and sailed into the top of the net. Under the most intense scrutiny for an individual player, Beckham produced a perfect move just when it was needed.

In 2003, Jonny Wilkinson produced a skilful drop goal in the dying seconds of the Rugby Union World Cup Final, which also demanded his ultimate skill.

People wanted to know how these two players were able to produce their absolute best when the stakes were so high. All successful people have an intuitive sense of their resourcefulness and their talents and how to develop them and apply them within their lives. David Beckham and Jonny Wilkinson gave us amazing examples of what can be achieved when resourcefulness is applied to talent.

To become more consciously aware of your natural talents refer back to Gardner's list of intelligences on page 31. Think about each one and pay particular attention to any thoughts that arise in your mind indicating a regret that you did not follow a career related to a particular type of intelligence.

Any feelings you experience in this area is your intuition speaking to you. Now is the ideal time to think into these feelings. Have you consciously repressed these feelings in the past or have they surfaced recently. This is your opportunity to rethink what you are currently doing to see if it aligns with your feelings about where your natural talent lies.

In summary:

- Your resourcefulness is different to your talent
- Your resourcefulness allows you to develop your talent
- Your resourcefulness may have been socialised out of you as you grew up
- You can re-access your resourcefulness at any time
- Your talents can be affected by the aging process but the potential of your resourcefulness remains infinite.

Exercise

1. What do you consider to be your talents?
2. Who or what would help you to develop these talents?

NEEDS

'All the evidence that we have indicates that it is reasonable to assume in practically every human being, and certainly in almost every newborn baby, that there is an active will toward health, an impulse toward growth, or toward actualisation [realising their personal potential].'
                                                                                            Abraham Maslow

Understanding human needs has been another driving force in the study of mankind since man started to think.

You may have come across Maslow's famous hierarchy of needs, first presented in 1943. Maslow said: 'What happens to man's desires when there is plenty of bread and when his belly is chronically filled? Other needs emerge and these, rather than physiological hungers, dominate ... and when these in turn are satisfied, again new (and still 'higher') needs emerge.'

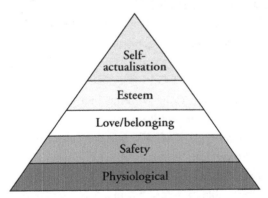

- At the base of the pyramid are our most primal needs, the physiological: the need to breathe, eat, drink, sleep, reproduce, excrete and keep the body in health
- The next level is our need to be safe: security of the body, mind and property

- The mid-level is our need for love and belonging: friendship, family, intimacy with a partner
- The penultimate is the need for esteem: the need for respect from others, self-respect, confidence and a sense of achievement
- Then comes self-actualisation: this covers the need for personal fulfilment, creativity, spontaneity, learning and growth.

Latterly he added another level, transcendence: the need for a sense of purpose and meaning by altruistically helping others.

There are many theories of needs and all the evidence shows that while we might act in irrational ways, we don't act randomly.

Erik Erikson's theory of psychological growth proposed that as we mature, our way of thinking changes; in other words, our needs change over time. People who buy bigger houses and bigger cars often do so to fulfil their need for status and recognition, not their core need of safety and security. An expensive restaurant habit might fulfil the same need, rather than the need for sustenance.

I was made redundant in 2001 and again in 2012. In that time the industry in which I had made my living had shrunk by about a third and there were new giants on the landscape: Google, Amazon, Facebook, LinkedIn. These companies weren't interested in people like me, they wanted those who were connected to the new generation coming through. So I found myself in a real dilemma; I didn't want to be one of those fighting for fewer and fewer senior positions in a fading industry, and I was tired of making people redundant. I wanted to be working in a growth industry where my days would be energising and fulfilling.

Doesn't this sound remarkably like someone from the millennial generation thirty to forty years my junior?

I came to realise that I had always felt that way about my career, but because I hadn't been able to describe it in a way that accurately represented my needs I wasn't able to pursue it purposefully. As a consequence the career path I followed was not fulfilling and meaningful for me.

Measuring our needs

Personality-profiling tools used in the corporate sector try to measure and represent the way in which people show behaviours as a consequence of trying to fulfil their needs. According to a neuroscientist friend, there are over 3,000 different profiling tools available. These tools can report on the likelihood of you being a good sales person, or the role that you might play in a team.

The tests generally categorise you into one of a number of possible personality types. By matching your profile to the profiles of many thousands of other people, they deduce the behaviours you are likely to demonstrate.

This type of analysis can help to explain behaviours, but it doesn't get to the root cause of why we do what we do.

What drives our behaviour

There is a predictable pattern to the things we do. These patterns change over the short term at a personal level as we grow and mature, and over the long term, perhaps as economic wealth and the security that comes with it allows a broader range of needs to be satisfied.

Our needs exist on a scale, so that it is possible for people to experience a need at different levels of intensity.

At university I studied psychology as part of my degree where I discovered an inconsistency in Maslow's hierarchy theory, that of the starving artist driven to fulfil their need for self-actualisation while neglecting the primal needs of physiology and security. Put simply they would forget to eat and sleep because they were so consumed by their work.

Some people have a very strong need for status and for others this matters little. Some need to understand how things work in minute detail before they can take on new tasks, whereas others can just jump in and get going.

I had a colleague who was always coming up with great ideas for new sales initiatives, but this was tied in with a strong need for recognition. If she didn't receive sufficient positive feedback she would sulk until she had moved on to another project and her mind became engaged again. Another colleague had a particularly strong need to connect with others. He was the life and soul of any meeting and his big personality would take over. I have a friend who has a highly developed need for excitement which he expresses in high-risk pastimes like cliff-diving.

I have also known people who didn't have a need to express their creative side in the workplace and kept it for their private life. They didn't crave public recognition, secure in their own knowledge that they were doing a good job at work. And of course there are many people who do not feel the need to engage in dangerous sports to rev up their lives.

I overheard a conversation at a business networking meeting. One chap was saying how he would never do business with someone who didn't have a nice car like a BMW because it was a sign of their success. This was a particularly sensitive subject for me because I was driving a rather old Ford. This chap's comments struck a chord because the car I drove had nothing to do with my ability to do my job. I was coming through a divorce and in the early stages of setting up my new business. For me, a shiny new car was irrelevant.

Experiencing the same needs at different levels makes communication harder

As George Bernard Shaw once said, 'The single biggest problem in communication is the illusion that it has taken place.'

If you enjoy jumping off cliffs or skiing the black run at Chamonix, you're going to find it difficult to understand the person who can't wait for the next version of *Warcraft* to be released, or the one who loves to curl up on the sofa and watch a movie with only a box of chocolates for company.

We punish or reward by withholding or giving what we know others need

As a species we are remarkable in many ways but one of our most amazing aspects is our unconscious awareness of the signals that other people send out and our ability to react accordingly. Children are particularly good at it. They unwittingly sense when a parent wants to receive a loving hug, but choose to give or withhold it at their whim.

Adults can behave in a similar manner.

Some years ago I was responsible for a hugely successful awards event that celebrated the role of small businesses in London. I wanted the top level of the company to know about this success – reflecting my need for recognition – so I emailed the chief executive, a man not known for his personal effusiveness. I didn't receive a reply. A week later the photos of the event came back and so I sent him a few showing me on stage with our celebrity political guests, some key members of staff and a few of the winners.

I got a reply this time but not the one I was expecting. The managing director popped his head into to my office and asked me to please stop sending emails to the chief executive. No well done, no congratulations, no recognition. In that instant, I knew my days at that company were numbered.

I'm sure you will be able to remember a time when something similar has happened to you at work, but in many ways it is most damaging when it happens in personal relationships and marriages. I only recognised that I had been guilty of this very trait in my own marriage when it was too late. If my wife did something to irritate me I would withhold some aspects of her need fulfilment that she was looking to me to provide. This sounds horribly callous but I only became aware of this behaviour after I started studying emotional intelligence, which was after the marriage had ended.

Once I became aware of this tendency I started to notice it everywhere: between friends, married couples at dinner parties, work colleagues, and children with their peers. What opened my eyes to this phenomenon was a book, *The 5 Love Languages* by Gary Chapman.

By the time my marriage was well and truly over I had started to date. Early into our relationship my girlfriend asked me to take an online test connected to this book, *The 5 Love Languages*. I felt every alarm bell go off inside my head. It took every bit of my self-control to say yes. The consequence was that I started to question our relationship. Although I really liked my girlfriend, I felt it was too soon to be talking about love. As she became more open in the way that she expressed her feelings, I began to withhold the very thing she was looking for that would fulfil her need to receive love. As you can imagine, soon afterwards the relationship finished. This sounds mean-spirited, but it wasn't a conscious act and I can only describe it with this clarity with hindsight.

Withholding your ability to fulfil someone's needs is something we do unconsciously, much of the time.

There are many reasons why we do this. It could be as a punishment in retaliation for a slight, because it can feel vulnerable to fulfil someone else's needs or we might be fearful of setting a level of expectation for the future

Need fulfilment creates new levels of need

You only have to go back a hundred years or so and look at old photographs showing women packing fish caught by their fishermen husbands … I don't know who was looking after the children, but their need to work to pay for their families' shelter and food overcame all other needs. Needs such as good-quality clothes, holidays and nutritious food were seen as luxuries only to be enjoyed by the 'haves' in society.

Sixty years later and the Second World War is over, the Western world seems a safer place, technology has driven industry and a new class is born. Those in the middle don't have as much as the 'haves' but they have a lot more than the 'have-nots' and they can start to fulfil more needs. They don't have to worry so much about a roof over their heads and food on the table. Now they can afford the paraphernalia of a modern life.

Fast forward to 2016. Many households now have two cars or more, the average family has more than one computer and many four-year-olds have a tablet to play with.

The more we have, the more we think we need.

This does not just apply to the material aspects of our lives. Once you have started to fulfil your need to express your creativity, you want more opportunities to be creative. When you finally receive recognition for your creative achievements, you crave greater recognition.

Think about a time you were asked to contribute to a new project at work, perhaps as part of a different team of colleagues. You joined in enthusiastically, pleased that your relevance had been recognised. In your mind you balance the extra demands on your time, and the consequence of spending less at home with your family, with the notion that your participation is an investment in your future security with your employer. But actually you enjoy the challenge of working with different people, experiencing new ideas outside of your normal responsibilities, and you like bringing the project to a successful conclusion and basking in the glory with the rest of the team.

Then you have to go back to your normal job, but it doesn't feel the same any more. Now you have more to give, you can contribute more, and, more to the point, you want to. You start to look around for opportunities that will enable you to fulfil your new needs.

Growth is a core human need, but as you fulfil it you also expand your capabilities and that stimulates other needs within you. This process creates tension as you try to balance the competing demands on your time and inner resources and the other responsibilities you have in your life.

This might seem like stating the obvious, but accepting it as a natural phenomenon can change the way you look at resolving the tension.

Needs play against each other to create inner tension

It would be lovely if our needs worked together in harmony and we could happily work towards satisfying those needs and experiencing a happy and fulfilling life. If only life was so simple.

When my children came along I wasn't prepared for the way I would feel about them. I knew I wanted to be a great dad, spending quality time with them and not missing those once-in-a-lifetime moments because of work.

The trouble was I worked in an industry that was not conducive to that way of thinking. Success came from developing a strong network of people who believed in you both inside and outside of the company. This required time, usually in the evening, going to networking events and being seen to be part of that community. This commitment didn't sit comfortably with the need I had to be a hands-on dad.

Because I didn't really understand what was happening, I felt that I wasn't doing my job as well as I wanted, plus I wasn't living up to the image I had in my mind of being the perfect dad. This inner tension became full-blown stress that I wrote off as just being part of the job I did. I wasn't able to see the effect this was having on me and the people in my life, both personal and professional.

It's important to recognise that as you develop and grow, internal conflict between your differing needs will create tension. This is a crucial step on the path to self-awareness. If you are a working parent, for example, you may experience this tension on a daily basis as you juggle your paid work, your parenting and your housework, not to mention your need for recreation and time to yourself.

It is our spiritual side that helps us deal with these tensions

Spiritual energy is the way in which we deal with the natural inner tensions that are a consequence of personal growth.

When we have tension caused by our needs pulling us in different directions it causes uncertainty. You can jump in, make quick decisions and accept the consequences, good or bad; you can put off decisions, otherwise known as procrastination. But there is a third option: to live comfortably with the uncertainty, with the unresolved tension.

The idea of living with unresolved tension can lead to a feeling of loss of control. Yet it is also the feeling of being out of control that is pulling so many people towards a more spiritual approach to life. People are turning to practices such as mindfulness, reiki, yoga and meditation as they look for ways to deal with the increasing tensions in their life and the consequence of increasing uncertainty. Being able to hold uncertainty and live comfortably with it is fundamental to a spiritual way of thinking.

Our stock markets lose or gain value because of market sentiment: the certainty or lack of it that investors have in the economy or in the fortunes of individual companies. How would the stock markets act if its players were able to live with their uncertainties?

Our education system is predicated on the idea that our children have to achieve an ever-increasing number of GCSEs so they can get a good job once their (formal) education is finished. How ironic that the youth unemployment rate in the UK and in many other countries is the worst it has been for twenty years. How different would our education system look if we were able to live with the uncertainty and give our children an education that truly nurtured their ability to think, rather than filling them with facts and theories that become redundant when they arrive in the real world of work?

We want certainty from our politicians, that the policies and laws they introduce will deliver the results they promise. When this doesn't happen, we end up with our policymakers baying at each other. How would the political landscape differ if we could all feel freer living with unresolved tension?

Delayed gratification of needs

Just ten years ago who would have known that most people would feel they had to have a laptop, a tablet and a smartphone? Today it can feel like our ability to survive in modern society is at risk if we aren't connected by all these devices – perhaps because they are tied up with our need for status and connection. When we are confused about how to fulfil our needs we may chase false solutions and then feel mystified when we don't feel fulfilled.

The delayed gratification of needs has been shown in many experiments to be a very reliable indicator of future success. It is our need for achievement that can derail us from a course where the payoff is some way off in the future. If the effort to achieve seems to be too challenging, then we can be tempted to take an easier path for a quicker result.

This was captured in the classic psychology experiment in the late 1960s and early 1970s led by psychologist Walter Mischel of Stanford University.

In it a marshmallow or other treat was placed in front of children sitting at a table. They had the option to eat the one marshmallow straightaway or if they could wait for 15 minutes they would get two. While the core results of how many opted to eat the marshmallow immediately and how many waited was interesting, what really made the research influential was the evidence that the children who were prepared to wait longer had more successful lives.

This is the principle of delayed gratification, our power to live with tension without the need to reduce or remove it. It takes practice and is part of the maturing process.

Displaying our neediness

When I was a young man my parents accused me of being too independent when I refused their generous offer to buy me a car. I remember having this very strong inclination that I didn't want to feel beholden to anyone. I was only to recognise the poverty of this way of thinking much later in my life. This was my way of displaying my need for independence, but I wasn't doing it in a very effective manner.

Unfortunately most people, in my experience, do not know how to ask for their needs to be fulfilled.

At a recent workshop on management and leadership I met a woman I'll call Jane who was having difficulty with an employee she was directly responsible for managing. Because she had been unable to resolve the issues, her line manager had stepped in, which had made Jane feel undermined and undervalued. As we talked I asked what she really wanted from the situation. She gave me what I call normal management gobbledegook – team harmony, good performance, etc. – so I asked her to be upfront with me. What did she really want from the resolution? Her honest answer was respect. She wanted respect from the person she was managing and respect from her manager. When we had isolated her overriding need, we were then able to talk about strategies she could use to help her achieve this. And I also talked to her about her ability to live with the tension and uncertainty if the situation didn't resolve itself in the way she hoped.

When we met again a couple of weeks later for the next workshop, the furrowed brow and tension had gone and she excitedly told me that she had resolved the issue. By getting clarity on which of her personal needs were being violated she was then able to understand why she felt the way she did and this enabled her to address the issue with her manager and staff member in a way that enabled her to get her needs met as she wanted. As a result when we met again she was feeling much better.

Needs are a natural consequences of being dynamic living organisms. The trouble is, for the most part we are not taught to be transparent about our needs but instead to subordinate them to the needs of others. When we are in relationships that don't fulfil our needs effectively we communicate our frustrations in subconscious ways, and a horrible spiral of miscommunication can lead to the destruction of what could have been a beautiful relationship.

Needs are always fulfilled

I have no scientific evidence to support this assertion, but I have come to this conclusion from personal observation.

If needs can't be fulfilled in a positive manner they will be fulfilled in a negative manner. It depends on the mindset of the individual. A positive mind will fulfil its needs positively and a negative mind will fulfil its needs negatively.

I was involved with a new start-up which was focussing on helping large organisations develop their corporate culture. One of the other members of the team had invested a lot of time and money in to developing the business concept and felt that his contribution to the business wasn't being recognised or honoured. He was feeling very unfairly treated by the other members of the team. As his efforts to remedy this situation seemed to be falling on deaf ears, in a final act of desperation he sent an email to all of the team describing the ways in which he had been unfairly treated and pointing out the individual shortcomings of the team.

He satisfied his need for justice by lashing out at his colleagues and in doing so ended up destroying those relationships and his connection to the business.

The needs

I have studied many different need theories and have distilled them into the following list. Included are descriptions of the positive and negative aspects of need fulfilment. They are not listed in any order other than subsistence and protection/security, physiological needs that naturally take priority over all the rest:

1. Subsistence
2. Security/protection

3. Health
4. Affection/emotional intimacy
5. Understanding
6. Participation/connection
7. Recognition
8. Leisure
9. Creativity
10. Identity/status
11. Freedom/autonomy
12. Meaning/purpose
13. Privacy/solitude
14. Competence/mastery
15. Achievement
16. Fulfilment
17. Excitement/risk.
18. Justice

Subsistence

This is our core need to eat, drink and breathe.

Positive: there is no over-consumption and the emphasis is on quality. The link between food and health is strong and there is an appreciation of the sensual experience of eating and drinking.
Negative: the watchwords are convenience and quantity. Pre-prepared meals, takeaways and highly processed foods are consumed without awareness or concern for their long-term effects.

Security/protection

Our need for security starts with a safe place to sleep and call home. It also encompasses our ability to earn money so we can create the life we want to lead and sustain.

The insurance industry has become expert at playing on this need by creating new products to cover every whim we have in the context of our need for security and protection. There was a time when retailers were making more profit from the insurance policies they sold to cover repair and breakdowns than they did from selling the products themselves.

Positive: the home represents a safe haven and is a place of enjoyment and relaxation.

Negative: the home is primarily a status symbol and is more associated with the need for identity.

Health

In Maslow's hierarchy our physiological needs are our fundamental drivers.

Physical health is reflected by the exercise we do and the food we eat.

The evidence is clear regarding exercise. The sedentary lifestyles created by most modern economic societies work against the natural maintenance of physical health and strength. So we have to consider our physical fitness and schedule it into our busy lives or the body starts to decline. Research carried out in 2013 by Bristol University showed that fewer than 10 per cent of the adult population in England walk for at least 5 minutes more than once a month. And nearly 80 per cent of people do not hit government physical activity targets of moderate exercise at least 12 times in a 4-week period.

When it comes to diet, there are basically four camps:

1. We should eat a balanced variety of foods as long as we don't over indulge
2. Processed food is the food of the devil and organically raised food is the only way to go
3. We should eat a vegetarian diet based on vegetables, fruit, nuts, seeds and grains
4. A meat- and dairy-based diet is what we have evolved to eat, and nuts, grains and seeds are biologically evolved not to be digested: the Paleo diet school of thinking.

I'm not a nutritionist and I wouldn't presume to give any advice in this area. Be conscious of which one of the four groups you are likely to belong to and just be aware of the potential consequences of your chosen approach.

Maintaining your physical health is a vitally important aspect of life and you ignore it at your peril. Physical health underpins everything you do. It provides the energy you need to take part in life the way you want to, from being effective and doing a good job at work to having enough energy for your family so you can enjoy their company.

Mental fitness is a much harder issue to discuss. There is no overall definition of good mental health that all health professionals concur on. The World Health Organisation defines it as: 'A state of wellbeing in which every individual realises his or her own potential, can cope with the normal stresses of life, can work productively and fruitfully, and is able to make a contribution to her or his community.'

In their report *What percentage of people in Europe are Flourishing and What Characterises them?* researchers Felicia A Huppert and Timothy T C So defined mental health as consisting of the following:

- Positive emotions: how happy you feel, engagement, having interests outside of yourself
- Relationships: having people in your life that you care for and who care about you
- Meaning and purpose: feeling that what you do in life is valuable and worthwhile
- Accomplishment: feeling that what you do gives you a sense of accomplishment and makes you feel competent
- Emotional stability: feeling calm and peaceful
- Optimism: feeling positive about your life and your future
- Resilience: being able to bounce back in the face of adversity
- Self-esteem: feeling positive about yourself
- Vitality: feeling energetic.

I believe that mental health comes from accepting the challenge of trying to satisfy our natural human needs, but recognising that they may not be satisfied to the extent we want. Mental health therefore lies in being able to hold the tension between our natural drive to achieve satisfaction, and the uncertainty that we will be able to do so. This explains why people can be happy in poverty and unhappy with wealth.

Exercise
What regular steps do you consciously take to maintain good physical and mental health?
How high up your list of priorities is looking after your mental and physical health?

Affection/emotional intimacy

Many people have such a strong need in this area that they will go from relationship to relationship in search of it. For some the prospect of being married is nothing more than a trap, limiting them from a bright and exciting world; for others it is the foundation of a deep and meaningful life. Is sex an expression of the love between two people or merely a physical need that requires satiating with whoever is available at the time?

It is difficult to write about this need without sounding judgemental and I would like to recognise that some people are able to have open relationships, but they tend to be a small minority. Across most cultures, with some noted exceptions, monogomy is the norm.

Positive: intimate relationships tend to be monogamous and partners support each other and live in mutual respect. Relationships are marked by high levels of trust, openness and the ability to work out conflicts.
Negative: one or both partners look outside of the relationship to satisfy their need for intimacy. The underlying trust is low, which leads to a lack of openness, and conflicts become difficult to resolve without causing lasting damage to the relationship.

The need to understand

The need to understand has been a fundamental driving force for human progress. Some people cannot do anything without having to know all the details first. Others have to know all underlying reasons. For example, one person in hospital might continually ask questions about their treatment, and another may prefer not to know.

Root-cause analysis is a technique to enable us develop our understanding, at a deep level, of why something is happening. It involves answering the question 'Why?' a minimum of five times, based on the notion that the first reason we come up with is usually a surface explanation and not the real reason.

If you are struggling to do or achieve something that you think is important, use this technique, but I would advise that you keep going and try and get to ten 'why's'. The more you uncover the harder it becomes to uncover the next 'why' and it requires you to go deeper inside yourself to get to the answer and therefore the understanding. This is a useful technique in many circumstances. For example, you might want to understand why you haven't been promoted, or why you can't stay calm when your children fight.

Positive: the need to understand is a natural part of our problem-solving brain. *Negative:* the need to understand can drive an unquenchable thirst for more information and can become a paralysing force. People in a position of power sometimes withhold information as an instrument of control.

Participation/connection

This is the fundamental need for us to be part of a group and to form societies. It's driven at a biological level. The hormone oxytocin, sometimes known as the love hormone, is triggered when we are with people that we like and feel connected to.

This is why we can feel sad and anxious if we have to leave a group where we have developed strong bonds. Think about the times you have left colleagues or neighbours. The need to belong is such a key driver of our behaviours that people who do not exhibit the need can become known as loners or misfits. The pull of the group can be so strong that we can find ourselves suppressing our personal needs in order to prioritise the needs of the group. Teamwork is often based on that very principle, which is why some people are able to work well in a team and others not.

Positive: the need for connection shows itself in healthy work relationships and friendships.
Negative: an overly accentuated need for connection can show itself in the relatively new syndrome FOMO, the fear of missing out. This may manifest in obsessive activity on social networks, and in the prioritisation of work and social events over family life.

Attention recognition

The need to be recognised for who you are as a person is a fundamental driver of many behaviours. It is closely linked to the need for identity and connection but is a separate need in itself.

Recognition gives us a sense of value and place within our society. In this context society could mean family, work, social life. We all have a need to be recognised by those we wish to associate with.

In its simplest form recognition can be conveyed by a thank you at an appropriate moment; but recognition can wear off quickly if it is not reinforced.

When I am training managers I always ask when was the last time they were thanked by their bosses and when was the last time they said thank you to their team? The answers are always enlightening.

The idea of recognition is embodied in most cultures through award systems. In the UK we have the Queen's honours and other countries have similar conventions.

It should be noted that monetary rewards are rarely successful as a means of showing recognition. To be effective, gestures of recognition should be personal and heartfelt.

Positive: recognition is given and received openly and honestly and unconditionally

Negative: recognition is used as a manipulative tool. This leads to a breakdown of trust and, ultimately, respect.

Leisure

From a scientific perspective it is undisputed that both the body and the mind need rest and recuperation to function at their best and this comes from making sure you create leisure time.

Jim Loehr and Tony Schwartz worked with high-level sports stars to understand the optimum balance between training, performing and recuperation. In their book *The Power of Full Engagement* they concluded that the recuperation period was just as important as the training in creating a great performance.

There is no prescription for what is the best way to recuperate, but it might not be your annual holiday. I'm sure you will remember a break that was more stress than relaxation and you were almost relieved to get back to work.

Positive: there is a clear link between leisure and bodily and mental recuperation. Leisure time is planned for and given priority.

Negative: the understanding of recuperation has been lost and the allocation of time to rest is seen as a waste. In this state, leisure time can create anxiety and the feeling that 'I should be doing something.'

> **Exercise**
> List ten activities that you enjoy doing.
> When do you give yourself the chance to recuperate?

The need to be creative

We all have the need to express our natural talent. Many will think of it in terms of the creative arts: painting, drawing, music, writing, acting. In recent years entrepreneurship has started to be seen as an expression of creativity. In fact, creativity is expressed in every type of human activity. There is creativity in writing the code for a new computer application, or in putting together a legal contract that is effective for all the parties involved. It can express itself in the creative care of a patient by a nurse or the nurturing of a student by a teacher.

Your creativity is the natural expression of the life force that is within each and every one of us. All human progress has come from people who were connected to their creativity as an expression of their life force. People who are connected to their creativity have energy, they have a sense of purpose and determination, and they exude a power that is not quenched by the doubts of others.

For this reason they can feel intimidating to those who have not connected to their creative life force.

The common theme of frustration for people in work is their inability to express their natural creativity. For some a lack of understanding of their natural creativity will lead them to follow careers on the basis of avoiding their frustrations because they have never stopped to investigate their creativity. Others will follow a path of what they believe they should do rather than what they feel naturally drawn to. When you are not connected to your natural area of creativity in your work, you will have to find an outlet outside of work in order to achieve a sense of creative fulfilment.

In my experience, managers can feel threatened when they see a good idea that was not originated by them. One of the biggest constraints on creativity in the workplace is that it gets pigeonholed into different areas. Watch the dynamics in a meeting when someone from purchasing tries to offer a new idea to the customer service manager, or when someone from finance tries to offer a helpful suggestion to a sales colleague.

In an organisational setting, creativity becomes siloed into areas of expertise. You have to earn your stripes in a given area for your ideas to be taken seriously.

Creativity is associated with change and can be a direct challenge to our need for security. So it becomes common for people to become very protective of their area of expertise and therefore their area of creativity and to dismiss the ideas of others.

Positive: you understand that creativity can be expressed in an almost infinite number of ways. When you are connected to your creativity as an expression of your life force it can be the most energising feeling in the world.

Negative: the negative manifestation of creativity is destruction and this can often be seen at play when someone, frustrated in the expression of their own creativity, will deliberately undermine someone else to prevent them from fulfilling their creative potential.

Exercise

Do you know your natural area of creativity?

Do you regard yourself as being creative?

The answer to this question cannot be no. If your instinct is to say you are not creative it is because you are not connected to your natural area of creativity, or you do not categorise your creativity as such because you have fallen into the trap of describing creativity as art or music or writing or sculpture or any one of the creative arts. If you have fallen into this trap, break out of it now.

A sense of your own identity/status

Our identity is constructed from an early age and built through the experiences we have as we mature. The key to understanding identity is the degree to which yours is created consciously or unconsciously.

Our identity consists of so many different aspects in addition to our physical appearance. It comes from the way we demonstrate our values, our level of self-belief and the beliefs we have about the world. Our identity is the ultimate expression of our personality.

Generally we feel pleased when people recognise and respect our identity, and our feathers get ruffled when they don't. For example...

One reason why many people find working in the corporate world difficult is the way it can demand the erasing of your own identity and the assumption of the corporate identity. But for others it becomes a means for them to express their identity as part of a group. The ultimate examples of this are the armed forces, the police and the fire and rescue service. In these services everyone espouses the same values and beliefs, and unity and direction are easier to establish and maintain.

The idea of authentic leadership was coined by Harvard professor Bill George in his book of the same name.

George interviewed hundreds of successful leaders and discovered that the key to their success was not following any formula or theory of leadership but applying effectively the learning from their life experiences and being authentic to that.

In his paper 'Counter-transference', published in the *British Journal of Medical Psychology*, English psychoanalyst D W Winnicott proposed the idea that we project a true self and a false self.

The true or authentic self is the self we feel most comfortable with and gives us our sense of enjoyment and pain that we experience from the world. Our false or adaptive self is like a protective mask we adopt if the things that give us enjoyment are not acceptable to the people around us. Do you have a guilty pleasure: music you like listening to or films you like watching but would never admit to your friends? This stops other people from seeing who you really are.

You can recognise when you are caught in your false self because it doesn't feel right. The giveaway signs are feelings of:

- Holding back and not saying the truth you feel inside
- Being closed to the truths that others point out to you. You can recognise this if you are particularly sensitive to criticism, easily hurt by things people say or rapidly feel anger rising within you
- Feeling constrained by the rules that other people (society) set.

We have an acute sense of when someone is not coming from their real self. It can be seen in people trying to be something they're not. But it can take time to discover your authentic self. Some people are lucky and feel in touch with it from an early age, and others can spend a lifetime and feel they still haven't discovered who they really are. Discovering your authentic self comes from having the courage to be honest with yourself and in your relationships.

Positive: your identity provides a frame of reference that enables self-confidence and the development of open, trusting relationships.

Negative: your identity can feel isolating and undermine your confidence. Self-image can become distorted and be the cause of disorders such as anorexia, bulimia and body dysmorphia.

Exercise
Do you know who you are and what you stand for?
Are you prepared to let others see that real you?

Freedom/autonomy

The human right to freedom and autonomy is the underpinning foundation of the principle of democracy, most famously captured in the American Declaration of Independence: 'We hold these truths to be self-evident, that all men are created equal, that they are endowed by their creator with certain unalienable rights, that among these are life, liberty and the pursuit of happiness.'

When your main concern is to keep a roof over your head and food on your plate it can be easy to demote the need for freedom and autonomy. In its ultimate form the removal of one's freedom is slavery, defined as the ownership of one human by another, but it also incorporates the idea of work without pay and atrocious working conditions.

It is always difficult to compare one period with another, but there can be no doubt that most people working in the seventeenth- and eighteenth-centuries would find it difficult to understand why there are so many complaints about conditions at work nowadays.

Inevitably freedom is bound up with wealth, but paradoxically in the modern developed world it is not always our jobs that create the feeling of entrapment and loss of freedom. It is the lifestyle we aspire to and the standard of living we have become accustomed to. It is not uncommon to sacrifice what we really want to do for what we have to do to maintain the living standards we have become used to.

This is captured brilliantly in the film *Good Will Hunting* where Matt Damon plays the role of a natural but unrecognised genius holding down a job as a construction worker, so he can be with his friends, until he is released from his self-imposed mental trap by psychologist Robin Williams.

If you have ever said to yourself: 'I can't do X because of my responsibilities' that is a symptom that you have not resolved your need for freedom and autonomy.

Positive: there is a good balance between your need for freedom and your need to be affiliated to others.

Negative: autonomy can express itself as the unwillingness to submit to any form of control, and at the other extreme, submission to the demands of another. It may manifest as the complaints of someone looking to blame everyone else for their circumstances.

Exercise
What does autonomy and freedom mean to you?
Are you living well with autonomy or do you feel trapped by life?

Meaning/purpose

It is purpose that gives direction and meaning to life. It is purpose that creates the 'fire in the belly' and drives you to take action. Purpose does not have to be big and grand, but without a sense of purpose, life can feel meaningless.

This is what Maslow was referring to when he added self-transcendence to his hierarchy of needs. Self-transcendence is the idea that we ultimately look to give ourselves to a higher purpose. It is a fundamental need of every human being to express their creativity and through that, to achieve their purpose and meaning.

In Daniel Pink's *A Whole New Mind*, connecting to your purpose will be the only way that people will be able to prosper, live a fulfilled life and enjoy the success they want in the future.

Positive: meaning and purpose are the result of expressing natural creativity. Having a sense of purpose creates a self-sustaining source of energy.

Negative: meaning and purpose is achieved through the control of others, whether this is at work or in personal relationships.

Exercise
Do you think you have a sense of purpose?
What does living a meaningful life mean to you?

Privacy/solitude

For some, total solitude is their chosen path and for others the idea of a moment on their own is challenging. Most of us exist somewhere between these two extremes. This aspect of our needs was really brought to the surface by the work of Carl Jung in identifying the characteristics of introversion and extroversion. These terms have come to be associated with people who are shy and not comfortable in big crowds and those larger-than-life characters who are the life and soul of the party. However, this was not the way that Jung defined introversion and extroversion.

For him they represented the mechanisms by which people recharged their batteries. Introverts tend to prefer more solitary pursuits whereas extroverts recharge by being with other people. The popular way of thinking about introversion and extroversion as being at opposite ends of the same scale is an inaccurate oversimplification. For some time the idea that business leaders needed to be very high on the extrovert scale has propelled some of the wrong people into positions they couldn't handle, and has also prevented introverts from reaching positions where they would have shone. The work of people like Susan Cain (author of *Quiet: the power of introverts in a world that can't stop talking* – you can see her talk on *TED.com*) is now challenging this old-style thinking.

Introverts have friends and like going to parties as much as extroverts but also like to have time on their own.

In fact, we all need some time on our own to reflect and to make sense of the things that happen in our lives. We can't do it in the company of others. Some marriages break down because one person doesn't understand their partner's need for privacy and solitude relative to their own. Some marriages thrive because both partners live separate lives and come together relatively infrequently, and others thrive because the partners spend all their time together.

Recognising your need for privacy and solitude and being able to respect others' needs in this area without becoming judgmental is key to developing your self-awareness and building relationships.

Positive: privacy and solitude provide quiet moments for self-reflection.
Negative: privacy and solitude can reflect a disconnection from other people and a lack of self-confidence.

Exercise

Do your needs for privacy and solitude complement those of the people you are closest to?

How often do you need the company of others?

Competence/mastery

There are limitations to what we can achieve. Just because I have a dream to become a 100-metre sprinter doesn't mean I have the genetic make-up to allow it to happen.

I used to be quite good at golf and by the age of fifteen I had achieved a handicap of 5. This brought me to the attention of those in charge of junior golf in North Wales and I found myself playing in the North Wales boys team with a certain Ian Woosnam. For those of you not familiar with the world of golf, Ian was to become the world number-one professional golfer, winning the US Masters Golf Tournament – one of only three British players in history to do so. I got to play with him once in a practice round at the Penarth course in South Wales, while preparing for the Welsh Boys' Championship.

One moment stands out in my mind as Ian stood on the tee of a long par 4 and hit his shot. I can still see the ball firing off the persimmon head of his club, sailing out for what seemed miles before landing in the middle of the fairway. But, more than anything, it was the sound that struck me as he hit the ball. I'd never heard anything like it before. In that moment my mind told me that I would never be able to hit a golf ball like that and I went from having mild aspirations of becoming a professional golfer to believing it was just a pipe dream, all in the moment of that beautiful shot.

In their book *Emotional Intelligence 2.0*, Jean Greaves and Travis Bradberry tell the story of a young man who wanted to play American football professionally. He was good enough to get through the college system and into a professional team, but he never got picked to start a game. He trained and dedicated years of his life to his obsession until finally the team coach gave him his opportunity. In a match that the team were winning comfortably and with only two minutes to go, the coach sent him on in an act of sympathy. His career finished immediately after his moment of glory as his contract wasn't renewed.

Was he right to spend ten years of his life training for two minutes of glory? The question that comes to my mind is, What else might he have done with those ten years? Perhaps training to become an American footballer gave him the experience he needed to be successful in a different career. This idea was played out in the film *Field of Dreams*. Doc Graham (Burt Lancaster) was a budding baseball player who had only one professional innings after years of preparation, before being sent down and retraining to become a doctor.

Sometimes we need to pursue a dream and fail so we can then discover our true area of mastery and success.

In his seminal book *Outliers*, Malcolm Gladwell popularised the 10,000 hours theory, originally proposed by Dr Anders Ericsson. It is the idea that masters of their professions engage in 10,000 hours of deliberate practice in order to reach their level of virtuosity. The world's superstars are those who know their area of natural talent and are prepared to put the work in to develop it to the level at which it becomes mastery.

Michael Jordan is one of the most celebrated examples of this idea. Having being rejected by his first-choice school, which didn't see his potential as a basketball player, it was only his determination and self-belief that finally enabled him to become the superstar we came to know. Similarly with Ian Woosnam: it would take him four attempts to win the professional card that allowed him to play the pro-golf tour, and some years after that before he had developed his game to the point he was the number-one-ranked golfer in the world.

Of course in a competitive world there is no guarantee that even if you match your natural talent to your determination to achieve mastery, you will become number one and achieve financial success. There are many factors that stand between talent and success.

This is the quandary in which many people find themselves. Do I pursue my mastery? Only you know what's right for you.

Positive: the need to achieve competence and even mastery is natural and when focused to an area of natural talent can be highly motivating and rewarding, but mastery is not a guarantee of financial success.

Negative: the drive for mastery can become obsessive and lead to a lack of balance in other areas of life. If unrelated to natural talent it can also be a source of growing frustration and disconnection to the people closest to you.

Exercise

What areas of your life do you think you have become competent in? What skills do you dream of mastering? How would you go about doing this?

Achievement

The need for achievement can be associated with risk and the need to push beyond your comfort zone. One of the barriers to fulfilling the need for achievement in the long term is the fixed mindset.

Those with a fixed mindset have a tendency to see achievement as a one-off big event that comes at the end of a journey of effort. Those with a growth mindset tend to see achievement as a process gained through a series of steps and marked by incremental progress.

The growth mindset approach is increasingly being adopted in the world of sports training. Those with the talent to be picked for the elite training programmes are given incremental benchmarks to achieve as signs that their training is taking them towards their goal. Inevitably, some people reach their physical limits before they get to the top level in their chosen sport, but others are able to achieve far beyond what they thought was possible.

One of the principles of this approach is the idea of celebrating success. It is easier to take a long and difficult path if you can celebrate each step taken towards your goal.

Positive: achievement is the result of effort applied effectively, especially in an area of natural talent.

Negative: the responsibility for results is abdicated so achievement can never be realised. Either effort is not aligned with natural talent and therefore results are never good enough, or resourcefulness is not applied to talent and so potential is never realised.

> **Exercise**
> Think about what the need to achieve means to you.
> What do you consider that you have achieved in the last ten years?

Fulfilment

Fulfilment is the need we all have to feel that the life we are living is worthwhile. If it doesn't, then freedom, autonomy, meaning, purpose, mastery and achievement count for nothing. It is the difference between that warm feeling of satisfaction and that cold empty feeling of 'What's the point?'

A recent Gallup survey into satisfaction in the workplace found that the general level of fulfilment in this area was worryingly low.

It was only when I had achieved a good standard of living that I began to sense a lack of fulfilment, and once that had come into my mind I couldn't get rid of it. I knew I wanted to do something that would be personally fulfilling. Then I found myself with the fear of losing the roof over my head and not being able to feed my family. The need for fulfilment suddenly seemed very self-indulgent and irrelevant and I settled back on the path of paid employment. This lasted until my second redundancy.

By this time my circumstances had changed substantially as my marriage had ended and I was no longer living in the family home. The one thing I knew for certain was that I wasn't going to chase another job working on projects that I didn't believe in and couldn't put my heart and soul into.

I decided to create a sales training business and as part of the development process I had come up with the line 'I help to take people's fear of selling away'. I booked myself on a business-development seminar. What I experienced that day would change my life for ever for the better and put me on the road I am now travelling.

It was the last presentation of the morning session. The speaker, who had created her own sales training company, took the stage. 'Hello,' she said, and introduced herself. 'I take people's fear of selling away.'

I felt like I'd been punched by the combined fists of Muhammad Ali and Mike Tyson.

I couldn't concentrate for the rest of her talk and can't remember what she said after those introductory words. At lunchtime I knew I needed to get out and think, so I went for a walk in nearby Regent's Park.

Doubts were flooding my mind: had I really created that line or had I just read it somewhere? But my overwhelming reaction was, why did I want to create a sales training company in the first place? The answer that came to me was that I was running to home, drawn towards the work I had been involved with for the majority of my working life. The real truth was I didn't enjoy it any more, even though I was relatively good at it; and it certainly didn't fulfil me.

As I walked back to the seminar that afternoon, I made the decision to drop the idea for the sales training business altogether. Instinctively I knew if I was to thrive rather than just survive, as I entered this new stage of my life, I had to be doing something that would be fulfilling emotionally, spiritually and intellectually, even if that came with no certainty of financial success (although that was another major need that I had to fulfil somehow).

Positive: fulfilment is the coming together of effort, applied to natural talent which has been developed to mastery, enabling us to truly express our creativity.

Negative: there is no connection between effort and meaning, so there can be no fulfilment. This occurs when we work in a job or career that has only one function: to pay the bills.

Exercise

Have you ever felt fulfilled?

If not, how will you know when you are?

Excitement/risk

'The need for the unknown, change, and new stimuli' is identified by motivational speaker Tony Robbins in his list of six core needs, which speaks to a very different aspect of our motivations than security.

For many, their reason for being is to analyse risk, calculate the odds of success, and if the reward is big enough, take on the challenge. In fact, risk can be found in every walk of life. It exists at the boundaries of our capabilities. Much of human endeavour is about the pushing of boundaries to discover just how far we can go, but this need for risk also plays against our core need for security, which is about the removal of risk and the creation of certainty.

Those who study risk will be quick to tell you that risk is not the same as reckless behaviour, which disregards the possible consequences. Excitement comes just before we overstep our boundaries of unreasonable risk. And because we all see the world differently, *we all have different risk thresholds.*

Financial advisors now have to ask us about our attitude to risk and get us to sign a document confirming they have diagnosed us correctly before they are allowed to prescribe their financial solutions.

Business leaders assess the risk of decisions on a daily basis, ski runs are designated different colours according to the risk they pose, and doctors talk about the percentage of risk involved in every operation. Risk is an integral part of living. To the extent that we choose the level of risk we wish to live with and bring into our lives it can be energising, but when we experience risk that is beyond our comfort zone it can create anxiety and, in the extreme, panic.

Positive: risk is an exciting part of life that provides opportunity for growth and personal development.

Negative: risk is avoided resulting in stagnation, or it is ignored resulting in reckless and ill-considered acts.

Exercise

What risks have you taken in your life?

Have you been reckless recently and if so, why?

Justice

I haven't met anyone yet without a sense of justice. We may have different opinions as to what represents justice, but it is what underpins the idea of a fair society.

Of all the needs it appears to be the one that is most affected by our need for safety and security. If we feel insecure in our job we are less likely to worry if someone else is being treated unfairly because our focus is on preserving our job security. But, if we come to believe that we could be subject to the same unfair treatment, then suddenly we become champions for the cause of fairness.

Children have a very well-developed sense of justice. From a very early age cries of 'it's not fair' can be heard because a brother got a slightly larger slice of cake or because a sister didn't get punished for committing the same misdemeanour. I remember the indignation of my son when he was nine because his friend had been told off unfairly by the teacher.

Of course ideas of justice vary and it stems from our individual perspectives and values. The most extreme expression of 'justice' is the death penalty. My own view is that this is not justice but social revenge, and herein lies the problem of trying to define what justice really is.

Positive: a strong sense of justice results in a mindset of fairness and compassion.

Negative: justice becomes more about revenge and reprisals for perceived injustices.

Exercise

Have your thoughts about justice changed since you were a child?

When did you last actively pursue your need for justice?

The influence of culture on our needs

Our needs are shaped by the culture, society and family we were born into. They evolve over time as we learn and experience more.

Most people are unaware of how their needs drive their behaviours.

Our ability to satisfy our needs is inextricably linked with our beliefs about the world and about ourselves. Understanding our needs and the tension that exists in trying to satisfy them is core to navigating the slings and arrows of outrageous fortune that life continually fires in our direction.

WISDOM

Q: What is Wisdom?
A: Wisdom is the ability to relate yourself to nature's laws so as to make
them serve you, and the ability to relate yourself to other people so as to
gain their harmonious, willing cooperation in helping you to make life
yield whatever you demand of it.

Napoleon Hill
Outwitting The Devil

Our wisdom has three aspects and none of them have anything to do with our knowledge of facts. They are our values, our beliefs, and our ability to embrace the natural laws.

Values

Your values are the standards by which you expect to live your life. For example, you might value honesty, loyalty, integrity or compassion. You receive your values from your parents and the societies you live in, like the inoculations you receive as a child. They are metaphorically injected into you starting from the day you were born. You acquire your values from the behaviours, views and opinions of your parents, teachers, friends, religious leaders and later in life, work colleagues and your national culture, and the accumulation of these values governs your behaviours through life. The values you have been taught form your expectations of other people and how you expect them to behave towards you.

In short, you can think of your values as the guiding principles by which you decide what you are willing and not willing to do.

And they are the reason that the teenage years are so challenging because this marks the period when we as individuals start to recognise our own power, and want to start living by our own values and not those handed down to us by those in authority. For some this is a very conscious feeling of rebellion, and for others it is a feeling of not fitting in.

As you mature into adulthood, your values develop into a complex mixture of those infused into you in your early years and those you choose to embody as a result of your experiences in life.

Beliefs

Your beliefs are what you hold to be true about yourself and the world around you. Our beliefs tend to exist as statements in our mind, such as: I'm no good at maths, I'm good at drawing, it's an unfair world, it's survival of the fittest. Your beliefs are developed through your own experiences of life, but many will adopt the beliefs of other key people in their life without testing whether these beliefs are actually true or not.

As with your values you build up your pattern of beliefs from birth. Whether your parents respond to your needs is the starting point for your beliefs about the world and your place within it. Over a relatively short period of time you establish a picture in your mind of whether the world is friendly or dangerous, whether people can be trusted or not and what you are capable of.

In short, your beliefs represent your picture of what you believe is possible for you in the world.

Natural laws

Natural laws are a body of principles that are considered to be inherent in nature and have universal application.

These laws exist at the boundary of what we are able to prove through scientific research and what observers over the millennia have seen about the way life unfolds in repeating patterns.

We know these laws intuitively at an unconscious level. It is only by bringing them into our conscious awareness that we can recognise when we are acting in harmony or in discord with natural law.

The laws of motion and the laws of thermodynamics are natural laws, as opposed to laws of man. Natural laws do not seek to favour or disadvantage anyone. They are a way of looking at the world that is not based on any one person's opinion of how the world or life works. They are the accumulated wisdom of many cultures over many thousands of years. It is your choice as to whether you see their relevance, or whether you remain subject to their influence without understanding how they work.

The idea that our lives are governed by invisible laws is a challenging concept but I am going to attempt to prove it to you. For instance, do you believe the following statement to be true or false?

Every thought you have, whether conscious or unconscious, manifests itself as a physical reaction in the real world.

Thoughts create emotional reactions that are translated into physical feelings in the body, such as butterflies in the stomach, a thumping heart or a tense neck. These physical reactions can be picked up by others through mirror neurons in the brain that have evolved to help us form relationships and recognise the feelings being experienced by another person. You will have noticed the effect of mirror neurons, or 'mirroring', if your body language subtly changes to mirror your companion's body language. Our thoughts also manifest as micro-signals in our facial expressions. We continually and unconsciously read the signals in others' body language, and in becoming of aware of another's emotional state our state changes.

From neuroscience – the study of the nervous system – we know that every thought we have is transmitted by a combination of electrical impulse and chemical messengers (neurotransmitters). These cause the creation of synaptic connections in the brain and, if thoughts are repeated frequently, will create new neural pathways. The opposite is also true. Where neural pathways have been created, the absence of reinforcing thoughts will cause those pathways to degenerate. You will recognise this if you have learned a foreign language and then not used it for some time. Those neural pathways are weakened as the brain transfers its resource to the areas that are more active. However, the brain can reactivate pathways when activity is started again and then your previous facility with the language will slowly return but much faster than if learning it for the first time.

This is the brain's evolved way of managing the resources it uses most efficiently and effectively.

An example of natural law in human affairs is that of giving and receiving. This is the foundation of all human relationships. Our professional lives are governed by this principle: I'll give you so much of my time and expertise in return for a salary and other benefits – healthcare, staff canteen, etc. We are relaxed with the idea of giving and receiving in a material context because there are usually clear rules. It might be a contract of employment, a contract of sale or even a marriage contract. Most contracts represent an agreed and binding understanding of reciprocal promises made between two or more parties.

As I tried to make sense of the breakup of my marriage and the role I had played in that, I came across the book *No More Mr Nice Guy* by Robert A Glover. His basic theme is that many people try to manipulate others to get what they want by being nice. (Although it is aimed at men, the principle is true for women as well.) As I read the book I remembered the many times I had adopted these manipulative behaviours and I cringed with embarrassment. But as I thought more about this type of behaviour, I started to see how inbuilt it is. As children we are told to play nicely. Underpinning Glover's book is a brilliant idea that transformed the way I saw myself and other people. It is the idea of covert contracts.

We all have covert contracts with other people and they exist in all aspects of our lives and go something like this:

If I do something for you, or if I give you my support in some way, then I expect something in return, although I'm not going to tell you what I want. If you don't give me what I expect, even though you don't know what it is, I'm going to feel hurt or angry or rejected or unappreciated and I'm going to punish you until you give me what I expect in return.

We have covert contracts with our partners, our children, our colleagues at work, our bosses. We even have them with our sporting heroes, film and pop idols, politicians and other influencers in our lives whom we haven't even met.

I came across another book, *The Go-giver*, by Bob Burg and John David Mann. Written as an allegory, it describes one man's journey of discovery in learning that you get what you give in life, and you have to be open to receiving what other people want to give or you block the giving and receiving process. This seemed like the fluffy new-age ideology that I had rejected all my life, but now I was opening myself up to the possibilities of a new way of thinking I started to see that everything we do in our relationships with other people is an act of giving and receiving, and like so many other aspects of life it happens at the unconscious level. These acts include: the giving and receiving of emotional support, love, care and compassion, and on the negative side, the giving and receiving of anger, frustration, nervousness, sadness.

In a horrible moment of insight I realised I had used my emotional state to reward or punish the people in my life, both personally and professionally. As the curtain of awareness raised, I remembered the times I had withheld my love, compassion and caring from my wife, my children and the people I had worked with and instead released my anger and frustration as punishments.

My feelings descended way below personal discomfort and embarrassment. I felt shame and entered a state of grief as I realised the role I had played in the downfall of my marriage and saw why my career had faltered. I was the cause, and I had received the effect.

I needed to understand more about this and my reading became much broader and diverse: in *Everyday Enlightenment* by Gyalwang Drukpa I discovered the concepts of attachment and detachment. I bought a personal development programme from John Assaraf (*johnassaraf.com*) in which he talked about natural law. This led me to Deepak Chopra and within his body of work I came across *The Seven Spiritual Laws of Success*, a guide to spiritual awakening.

I'd come to a new understanding about the role of giving and receiving and how that had impacted my life, so I embarked on another line of research to see if I could establish a list of natural laws. I have listed these overleaf (not in any order of priority). These natural laws cannot be felt at a physical level, and without bringing them into your conscious thinking you will not be aware of the effect they have. But just as surely as gravity keeps you safely on the ground, these natural laws are affecting you. The laws are constantly in play and they work together inextricably.

The list of natural laws developed here has come from the study of philosophical and spiritual writings of both Eastern and Western cultures. They form a reference point against which we can benchmark our experience of life and make sense of the results we achieve, independently of the experience of someone else. They are opinion neutral.

I would give yourself time to fully absorb the meaning and implications of each law. What I came to realise is that it is conscious acceptance of natural law that will enable you to live to your potential. Each law is described with examples and includes *Contra-signs*:

These are the clues that indicate you are not working in harmony with the natural law.

1. The law of action and reaction
2. The law of cause and effect
3. The law of detachment
4. The law of gender
5. The law of gestation
6. The law of giving and receiving
7. The law of growth and decay
8. The law of intention
9. The law of Intuitive Success
10. The law of polarity
11. The law of potential
12. The law of purpose
13. The law of relativity
14. The law of rhythm
15. The law of the perpetual transmutation of energy
16. The law of vibration

The law of action and reaction

Sir Isaac Newton was the first to recognise this law in the physical world and its description is his third law of motion: 'To every action there is an equal and opposite reaction.'

Nothing happens without an action, an obvious statement but one that many do not understand. Intention is the necessary mindset to take you forward, but it has to trigger an action for things to happen. Intention without action is just wishful thinking and it will keep you rooted in your current circumstances.

All actions create an equal and opposite reaction. In the physical world it is the principle by which we get rockets to fly. It is the jet of the combustion gases forced out backwards from the rocket that propels the rocket forward. This same principle applies when you push against a brick wall; the harder you push against the wall, the harder it resists your efforts, otherwise you would just be able to push it over. It is the bonding force of the mortar holding the bricks together that enables the wall to resist your push, but the key concept to grasp is that the wall is actively resisting your efforts to push it over. Hence your action is creating an opposite reaction.

This resistive force applies to your creativity, the expression of your life force. Intention will take you to the boundaries of your abilities and experience and it is at this point that your fears and doubts will be triggered. These fears and doubts represent your brain's reaction to your intended actions. It is its natural role to keep you safe when it unconsciously perceives a threat.

What marks truly successful people out is their ability to push past their fears and doubts and take action. You will need a growth mindset that allows you to learn from mistakes and to see failures as the opportunity to learn and try again a different way. Nelson Mandela famously said: 'I learned that courage was not the absence of fear, but the triumph over it. The brave man is not he who does not feel afraid, but he who conquers that fear.'

Those with a natural instinct to take action and the supporting mindset to learn do not see themselves as being particularly brave or courageous, whereas those with a fixed mindset or with no awareness of natural law will often look on in envy as they see others take their lives forward in new and exciting directions.

Action is the foundation of Susan Jeffers's famous book *Feel the Fear and Do It Anyway*, and probably the most famous of all brand slogans is Nike's 'Just Do It'.

Our mind likes to hold on to the idea that if all the ingredients are right then action will lead to the result we want, but it is very rarely the case that we have all the right ingredients at the right time. Taking action requires that you accept uncertainty and make your move before all the pieces of the jigsaw are in place.

Contra-signs:

You feel there's always a reason why it's not the right time to take an action that you really want to take, whether it is going on a diet, changing jobs, finishing a relationship, starting a business or asking someone out for a date. When you only allow the 'reaction' part of the law to be dominant you will never take actions that will take your life forward.

> **Exercise**
> Think about what action you would really like to take right now.
> Ask yourself, What is the first step I could take as my first action?

The law of cause and effect

This is the law of personal responsibility. It requires you to accept that it is your thoughts and the actions that result from them that is the major factor in influencing the shape and direction of your life. There are very few people who truly take this law to their core. The main reason for this is the fact that there are events happening regularly in our world that are beyond our control.

An undersea earthquake causes a massive tsunami to travel thousands of miles, wreaking havoc in millions of lives. Were any of victims responsible for this awful occurrence in 2004? Of course not, but each person had the option to respond in a number of ways in the aftermath. Two planes were deliberately crashed into a building in New York in 2001. Were the victims or their families responsible for this disaster? No they weren't – but the survivors had the freedom to make their own choices, within the context of their new circumstances, after the event.

The work of Viktor Frankl and Martin E P Seligman has shown us that by consciously taking responsibility for the way that we respond to the events in our life, we can make dramatic differences to the long-term outcome of short-term events that are beyond our control.

The trouble is that one of our core needs tends to kick in when unexpected events take us to a place we hadn't intended to go: the need for justice. This can make us look for scapegoats to blame for our misfortunes and so deflect the responsibility of the long-term consequences from ourselves.

Contra-signs:

When you start looking for causes outside yourself for the events in your life. Remember this is about blame and absolving yourself from responsibility. First, it is a very disempowering approach: you are saying there is nothing you can do about your circumstances. This may relieve your anxiety or feelings of injustice in the short term but in the long term will prevent you from taking positive steps to recover. Those who work against the law of cause and effect come across as victims, either intentionally, as an attempt to garner sympathy for their plight, or unintentionally as they display their helplessness. They can also come across as very forceful as they look to deflect attention from their own shortcomings.

The blame state has a low vibrational energy (see the law of vibration) and it will repel those with a high vibration who are the very people who can help. Responsibility is a high vibrational state and if you accept the law of cause and effect, you will naturally rise to this higher vibrational level and start to attract similar energies to you.

The law of detachment

The law of detachment flies in the face of modern Western thinking. We live in a world where we are told we have to be passionate about what we do. Employers want passion from their employees, fans want passion from their sports and film stars, we demand passion from our politicians.

I remember a headline in the jobs pages some years ago that made me laugh out loud: 'Are you passionate about street furniture?' – street furniture being things like bus stops and signs that tell us to keep off the grass. How could be anyone be passionate about that? Some time later I realised it was exactly the right headline. Of course there would be someone out there who was passionate about street furniture.

Passion has become the buzz word for recruiters and employers trying to identify the ideal candidate, and for those trying to articulate how strongly they feel about a subject.

We need passion in our lives. It provides excitement and drive and it is part of the essence of being human that we can feel such a level of emotion. However – we can become overly attached to whatever we are passionate about.

In fact, it is difficult to think of being passionate without the associated feeling of attachment. When you are attached to something, it drives your behaviours to protect and defend. Passion can trigger a narrowing of focus and a loss of perspective.

We become attached to ideas, possessions and people because they are part of what gives our lives meaning. When we have meaning we don't want to lose it, so we do everything we can to protect it, and we become attached to it.

The 'brains' of the financial world had convinced themselves that they had created financial products (derivatives) that enabled risk to be hedged and effectively removed from the banks' balance sheets. They were so attached to this idea that they couldn't see the truth until it was too late.

We can become attached to people to the point that we can't see it is a bad relationship.

In this attachment are the seeds of destruction of the very thing we are trying to protect. Attachment is part of our need for certainty (protection/ security). We want to know that the investment of time, effort, love, money or whatever else we put into our passion will be worth it, that we will get back at least as much as we put in.

But life isn't like that. There are no guarantees that things will turn out the way we would like. So it is only in detachment that we can stay open to the possibilities of life. Detachment allows your focus to stay broad and for you to hold different perspectives at the same time. It enables you to accept the uncertainty that is inherent in existence.

Detachment is anathema in a world driven by money where investments have to yield a return or heads will roll. Where we demand that every box of Kellogg's cornflakes looks the same and tastes the same. Where we demand that our apples come blemish-free and similarly sized.

This is because we misunderstand the nature of detachment, which is not the same as being emotionally detached and unfeeling. Many people actually resort to emotional detachment as a coping tactic. They can't deal with emotional rollercoaster rides so they cut their emotions off. But this is not true detachment.

True detachment comes when you give freely of yourself in all aspects, with no expectation of return and with the ease of allowing the uncertainty of events to emerge without the need to control them. For example, you might fall in love with a new partner; it is only in detachment that the relationship can flourish. Detachment allows each partner to grow and develop into their full potential. If we are attached to the other person the tendency is to want to keep them as they are and this is when many relationships start to fail. It is important to recognise that we are not talking about emotional detachment. The ability to be detached but in touch with your emotions is the ultimate expression of love.

In detachment lies freedom, both for yourself and for the people in your life. Detachment creates an ease of living which is palpable. It doesn't imply any loss of passion in any aspect of life: in fact you can become more passionate in detachment because the pain of loss and uncertainty are diffused.

You can recognise how attachment feels when you hear yourself saying things like, 'I will be happy when I meet my next serious partner/I publish my novel/I lose a stone/I get a new job'. The 'when' is the attachment trap we can all fall into. Attachment keeps you locked into what you know and stops you from seeing the possibility, the opportunity and the learning that exists for you.

Remember, detachment is the key to freedom and opportunity, learning and growth.

Contra-signs:

The signs of resistance to the law of detachment show up as the consequences of a clear attachment to a specific outcome. They can include:

- Feeling hurt by imagined slights from family, friends and work colleagues
- Irritation with people when they don't do what you want
- Sense of personal failure and loss if things don't work out the way you would like
- An inability to learn the lessons of life and repeating the same mistakes over again
- Fear of nurturing growth in others for fear they will no longer want, need or love you.

The law of gender

I am totally indebted to a wonderful woman, Dr Hamira Riaz, for helping me to really understand this law. We met a couple of years ago and in truth I do not know her that well, but we met again recently for a coffee and she was to change the way I look at the world. Hamira is a neuro-psychologist who has probably forgotten more about how the brain works than I'll ever know. She is the epitome of the Law of Gender at play. She is a true force of nature: enlightened, passionate and determined.

The law of gender is rooted in the Hermetic philosophy and tradition which can be traced back to Ancient Greece and Egypt. *The Kybalion*, published in 1912, put forward a number of principles including the principle of gender. This is the idea that there are inherent male and female qualities, and that we only reach our full potential when we allow both aspects of our selves to be expressed. The trouble is that this aspect of our creative expression is trivialised and undermined on a daily basis by the stereotypes that society has created for the roles we play.

When distilled to its purest idea, the law of gender states that creation only occurs with the coming together of the masculine traits of will and power and the feminine traits of imagination and potential. Will and power exercised with no connection to imagination and potential leads nowhere productive, as does imagination and potential not imbued with will and power.

History is full of examples of men known for the expression of their imagination and potential: Gandhi, Wilde, Dali, Picasso, Martin Luther King, Darwin and Einstein, and it is full of examples of women who are known for the expression of their will and power: Cleopatra, Boudicca, Joan of Arc, Evita Peron, Margaret Thatcher, Madonna.

Increasingly, gender stereotypes are being broken: for example, more men feel able to be the stay-at-home parent while the woman takes on the breadwinner role. But the law of gender is much more significant than that. At the most fundamental level we need the male and the female aspects for life to exist. It is politically incorrect in today's world to talk of inherently male and female qualities, but biologically male and female behaviour is driven by different hormones. Men by testosterone and women by oestrogen.

You might be familiar with examples in your friends or colleagues of men who are not comfortable showing their caring and compassionate side, and of women who lead downtrodden lives because they find it difficult to embrace the masculine qualities associated with assertiveness.

It is the law of gender that allows us to be assertive and compassionate at the same time. When you are fully engaged with your male and female qualities you become a force of nature. One of my favourite lines from the book *The Fountainhead* by Ayn Rand: 'The question isn't who is going to let me? It's who is going to stop me?'

Contra-signs:

Resistance to this law manifests as an under or over-expression of emotion and a lack of balance in personal qualities. The signs are:

- not being able to forgive and move on
- the acting out of intolerable behaviour
- the acceptance of intolerable behaviour
- lack of empathy towards others or an overly sympathetic response to the difficulties of others.

The law of gestation

The law of gestation states that everything happens in its own time. For example, if you want to grow an oak tree you have to plant an acorn. Depending on the species and provided it has been planted with the right conditions it will sprout in approximately forty days, but some oak trees take nearly a century to reach their full height. There is no way round it. You can't make an oak tree grow any quicker. If you can't wait a hundred years, you could plant bamboo and have a very substantial bamboo plant within a few years, but it won't be an oak tree.

There has always been resistance to this law. It has reached a peak in recent years as the lure of overnight success created by TV shows such as *The X Factor* and *Britain's Got Talent*, *The Apprentice* and *Dragon's Den* have lured people into the illusion that you can create success overnight. You only have to follow the fortunes of the winners of these shows to see this principle at work. It takes time and the right conditions to create a successful career or business. Some go on to create long-term careers after their moment in the spotlight, but the majority do not. This is because there is no such thing as overnight success. The truth is that most people who appear on reality shows want instant fame and glory and only a few have the determination to develop their talent over time, allow their potential to evolve and ultimately realise their dream.

It was the ignoring of this law that created the dotcom bubble of the late 1990s when billions of pounds and dollars were invested in internet ideas that were founded on nothing but the dream of getting rich quick.

The right idea, at the right time, developed and nurtured in the right way can create big success relatively quickly – Google, Facebook and Amazon are testimony to this – but they still followed the law of gestation.

Virginia Satir, an American family therapist, developed an approach in which she identified the processes through which change happens in most people. The Satir Change Model has become widely adopted in the business world.

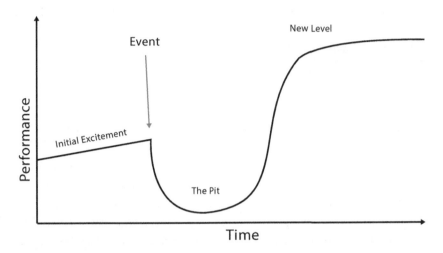

What her model shows is that the path to success is not a straight line, and that we have to invest a lot to overcome the challenges of life to get to the point that we call success. When you understand this process you can recognise its presence in every aspect of life, from every new relationship, new business, new job, new product – every challenging event in your life.

In summary, every new project takes its own time to reach maturity or, to put it another way, some things take longer to come to fruition than we would hope.

One of the difficulties is that we only get to hear about success after the event. Which means we rarely get to hear about the period of gestation it has taken to become successful.

Contra-signs:

A lack of understanding of this law leads to:

- Impatience
- Taking imprudent risks

- Unrealistic expectations of immediate results
- A lack of perseverance and determination

Exercise

1. Do you have a new relationship/career/project that is important enough to you for you to stay with it and invest in it until it reaches maturity?
2. Do you have the patience to nurture it until maturity?

The law of giving and receiving

Understanding the mechanism of giving and receiving is fundamental to living at your full potential.

We usually think of giving and receiving at the material level, but the principles apply in everything we do. Whether it is the giving and receiving of friendship, love and support or anger, hate and impatience, we are in a constant process of giving and receiving. We are taught that it is good to give and that we should be grateful for what we receive, but there is so much more to it than that.

Giving, by its very definition, implies that you receive nothing in return. If you expect something in return it becomes a trade, and the aspect of giving is gone.

I challenge you to think very hard about every aspect of your life and make a list of what you truly give without the expectation of a return on it. Do you love your partner without expecting their love and commitment in return? Do you love your children without expecting their love in return? Do you give support to your friends without expecting their support in return?

The key word here is expectation.

In his book *Predictably Irrational*, Dan Ariely uses the example of a primary school that had a problem with parents arriving late to pick up their young children at the end of the school day. The school's relationship with the parents was generally good but their lateness to pick up was putting extra pressure on the teachers. In order to solve this problem the management committee decided to start fining parents who came late, assuming they would not want to receive a financial penalty.

Unexpectedly, the exact opposite happened. Even more parents started to turn up late. The financial penalty changed the relationship from one of mutual trust to a transaction. Parents started calculating that the cost of the fine was worth the extra time. In effect they regarded it as a cost of child-care. When the school's management committee imposed the fine they had stopped 'giving' and the nature of their relationship with the parents was changed for ever.

It is our expectations around giving and receiving that affect the nature of the act, not the act itself. I am not suggesting that you should stay in an unfulfilling relationship where your love is unrequited. The point is that you should give your love without expecting any in return. A truly successful partnership emerges when both partners understand this and feel free to give their love. When you expect love in return it ceases to be love freely given and in that loses its meaning and power.

Most cultures teach that giving is better than receiving, but have you ever thought about what happens when you block someone else trying to give to you?

Think about times you have rejected the love of your partner or children even if it was just for a fleeting moment. What effect do you think that had on them?

Have you ever rejected someone else's well-meant advice? Because we all have a difference experience of the world, we assume that other people don't understand what we have been through. How could they? They don't have our experience. That is why we sometimes reject advice or support, but in rejecting someone's efforts to help us we are also resisting their efforts to give.

If we continually reject what other people want to give to us eventually they will stop giving.

You can only truly experience what you give, not what you receive.

I ask you to re-read this until you understand, at your deepest level, its full significance.

The nature of giving often means that we are challenged to give of our-selves in the very moments we do not feel like giving. If we are irritated we are unlikely to be patient with the person who we feel is the cause of the irritation. If we have been hurt by a loved one or a friend we are unlikely to feel like showing our love in return.

But these are the moments when we can truly experience those feelings by giving when our instinct is to withhold.

You cannot receive what you do not have to give.

If you are closed off from your feelings of love, for example, you won't recognise the potential for love when it comes into your life and you will not be able to feel and experience it yourself.

Take some time to consider this idea because it is a fundamental principle of life.

Whatever you want to experience in life, you first have to be able to give it: freely, willingly and without the expectation of anything in return.

Contra-signs:

- The closed demeanour of someone who is difficult to get to know
- A suspicious nature and lack of trust
- An eye-for-an-eye mentality, seeking revenge for perceived slights

The law of growth and decay

If there was one law I wish I had understood earlier in my life it would have been this one. This law acknowledges that life exists in a struggle between growth and decay. If something is not growing, then it is in a state of decay. The laws work to create harmony between these forces of life and death. When a living thing stops growing it starts the process of dying and, when it has died, decays into its constituents which then become available for other life forms to use.

Up until a few years ago economists used to talk in terms of inflation and deflation, but more recently they have referred to positive and negative growth. This is a very useful term when considering how our brains work and the way in which we grow as people.

The law of growth and decay reflects Carol Dweck's concept of different mindsets. The growth mindset accepts we are not perfect, we can learn from failure and that effort expended to master new skills is a good investment. A fixed mindset finds it hard to accept imperfection, regards failure as a judgement about one's capability, and effort spent on training as a risk because there is no guarantee that you will master new skills.

The person with the growth mindset will have their experience of growth constantly reinforced by the brain as they take on new challenges and responsibilities. We can think of this as positive growth. The person with a fixed mindset will experience the opposite. Their neural pathways will be strengthened in the area of the brain relating to their experience of failure. Growth has happened but in a negative direction.

As living beings, we experience life through our tendency to grow and this can be experienced in the positive or the negative. Growth will happen whether you are consciously part of the process or not, but how you grow will be determined by whether your mindset is growth or fixed. Becoming conscious of whether your growth is positive or negative is key to unleashing your potential. Achieving true success is only possible when you recognise a habit of negative growth and remove it from your habitual thoughts.

Contra-signs:

- Someone stuck in their ways and unable to accommodate alternative opinions or views of the world
- Feelings of disempowerment and frustration
- Lack of personal fulfilment
- The feeling of unrealised potential within
- Sustained negativity

Exercise

Can you identify any areas in your thinking that represent negative growth?

Have you made any big changes in your perspective on life, moving from negative to positive?

The law of intention

To understand how this law works you have to understand the nature of intention. Intention is not wishful thinking, it isn't about saying to yourself time and again that you want to be successful. It is not about writing your goals down in a list. In short, the law of intention is about becoming the living embodiment of what you want. In so doing you move out of the state of wanting and into the state of being. This is a much bigger commitment than holding a number of wishes, dreams and ambitions in your head.

When you enable the law of intention within you, your energy level changes and sets in train a flow of events that will ultimately help you to create what you want in your life. You know when you are dealing with someone of intention rather than someone who has wishes. There is a different level of intensity about them and they can appear as an unstoppable train. And yet, intention on its own doesn't guarantee success, so it has to work with all the other laws to guide you towards your achievement.

One of the obstacles for many people is the idea of time. We are impatient and we are jealous. When you have a great idea you want that idea to come to fruition quickly and you look at the success of others and say to yourself, why can't I be as successful as them? The second that these negative thoughts enter your mind, your focus and attention has moved from your intention and your energy is no longer directed at your goal.

If there is a law that is likely to challenge you and provoke your resistance to the concept of natural law, it is this one. It goes against everything that we are brought up to believe: that our hard work will be rewarded and that we can control the results we achieve.

Control is a concept that comes from a fixed mindset. The law of intention is part of a different way of thinking. When you create the right conditions by activating a conscious acceptance of natural law within you, the results you want are an irresistible by-product of your intention and will flow through you subject to the law of gestation, which says that everything happens in its own time.

When I was at university a friend of mine had one and only one ambition: to join one of the major FMCG companies in the world. He knew the company and the role he wanted within it. He ate, slept and breathed his dream for three years; he was the living embodiment of the law of intention. Needless to say his dream came true.

Contra-signs:

- Aimlessness and lack of direction
- Lack of ambition
- No drive or energy
- Lack of purpose

Exercise

Can you identify a goal that you didn't achieve in the timeframe you had earmarked and as a result, you let it go?

What did you learn as a result of your investment in that goal that will help you to achieve a new goal?

The law of Intuitive Success

Do you believe that success should come naturally to you? Or do you believe that success only comes through hard work?

How do people like Michael Jordan, Richard Branson, Yo-Yo Ma, David Beckham, Alan Sugar, Damien Hirst and Brian Cox achieve their success? Yes, they work hard, but that in itself is not the answer.

You will recall that one of our core human needs is to express our natural creativity. The law of intuitive success states that when we apply our need for mastery and achievement effectively in line with our areas of natural talent and aptitude, then we are in our place of intuitive success.

The signs of being in your place of intuitive success are:

- You agree with the sentiment: 'When you do what you love you never work a day in your life'
- You understand people who find their work energising
- You can relate to people who give up an evening out because they want to practise and develop their skills

Your place of intuitive success was identified by Hungarian psychologist Mihaly Csikszentmihalyi as being a state of flow. In essence, flow is characterised by complete absorption in what one does. The opposite of flow is being engaged in activities that literally sap your strength.

Your area of intuitive success lies in identifying an activity that is a natural strength and represents an aspect of your natural creativity that you enjoy investing time in to master, and which makes you feel energised and excited. This law doesn't mean you don't have to work hard. It means that when you apply hard work to the talents that allow you to express your natural creativity, success in some form will follow.

There is a famous quote often attributed to Einstein: 'Everybody is a genius. But if you judge a fish by its ability to climb a tree, it will live its whole life believing that it is stupid.'

It is an unfortunate consequence of the way that most of us are educated and trained in the workplace that we look at what is not working well and then focus our attention on fixing those aspects. In business this is a very necessary process to make sure an organisation is functioning at its best, but when applied to the individual it can result in misdirected effort and a wasted opportunity to develop latent talents.

Please watch the TED talk by Sir Ken Robinson on this subject (*https:// www.ted.com/speakers/sir_ken_robinson*). It is the most important of all TED videos because it addresses the fundamental issue of how we educate our children and prepare them to become adults.

Contra-signs:

- Living your life based on what you think you should be doing, rather than allowing your natural interests and abilities to determine your path
- Working at improving weaknesses rather than developing strengths
- Lack of enjoyment at work
- Feeling unfulfilled

The law of polarity

The law of polarity is the idea that everything has a polar opposite. It is about tolerance and diversity and accepting that not everyone will agree with you, like you or want to be part of your world. Some people are more comfortable with this idea than others. For example, the pleaser is well-meaning and wants to please everyone, but the principle of this law means that cannot happen and you will no doubt have met someone who does not seem to care about anyone else.

The law of polarity says that one thing cannot exist without its opposite. Its symbol is the yin and yang, a complementary, interconnected and interdependent symbol. One cannot exist if the other does not exist. So, without failure we would never experience success. Napoleon Hill said: 'Every adversity, every failure, every heartache, carries with it the seed of an equal or greater benefit.'

The law of polarity has been embraced in the world of marketing and advertising and is referred to as 'the Marmite principle'. If you want to have a successful product you have to identify who will like your product and direct your marketing specifically at those people and accept that there will be a significant number who will not be attracted. Apple applies this principle most effectively and as a result has a worldwide army of adoring fans but equally has as many who do not like their products or what they stand for.

The law affects the natural world; for example all foods have the potential to be nutritious or poisonous. For instance, the berries of the mistletoe and holly bush are toxic to us but birds love them. New research is suggesting that the so called super-foods blueberries and goji berries contain chemicals that can exacerbate conditions like asthma and arthritis. There have been cases of people dying from intoxication after drinking far too much water after taking the drug ecstasy.

This law expresses itself in some of our most primitive biological programming. For example, our fundamental need to be part of a group made up of people similar to ourselves. This basic drive has led to some of the most barbaric acts in human history, to ethnic cleansing and acts of war. It comes from the fear and distrust of people who are not like us and is still a force in the world today.

Understanding this law is fundamentally important as the seeds of success can be found in the core of failure, but only for those who understand this natural law.

Contra-signs:

- Intolerance towards others
- Not realising the potential of working with others of a different point of view
- Not understanding your role in the world and the unique contribution you have to make

The law of potential

An acorn has the potential to become an oak tree. With the right conditions it will achieve its potential of becoming an oak tree.

Without accepting the law of potential, and our belief in ourselves to create a different future, we remain stuck where we are. We love overnight-success stories but apart from those lucky few who win the lottery (and would you really count this as success?) I have never come across a success story that wasn't based on a journey of growth and belief, where the hero of the story hadn't had to overcome many hurdles before realising their true potential. We have to be able to create the right conditions for germination and growth.

There are genetic limitations to the potential we have in some areas of life and genetic advantages in others. For example, Michael Phelps was able to become the most successful swimmer in history because of his unique body construction: hugely long arms, long torso and short legs and unusual lung capacity. He came from the ideal physical mould for a swimmer but it was the determination, dedication and perseverance he applied to his physical attributes that enabled him to become a phenomenon and achieve the potential that lay inside him.

Potential is latent within all of us but it requires conscious will (remember the law of intention) to activate it, and an understanding of the journey that follows for potential to be realised. For some their instinct for their potential becomes a resolute driving force. Others struggle to feel their inner potential but never lose the feeling that there should be something more … if only they could find it.

My daughter's natural ability in art is a source of amazement to me. From an early age she has been entirely happy spending hours drawing, in a state of flow. My friend's inner passion was music and for a time he enjoyed the success and glamour of life in a pop group. The pop career faded but his love of music never has and he talks of friends he has who just 'have to play'. It was what they were born to do.

But how do you seek out your natural talent, your natural creativity, if it is not obvious to you or anyone else?

This can be a challenge and is very much related to our self-belief.

I would like to introduce you to an idea that you might find difficult to accept: Your mind is trying to tell you about and guide you towards your natural talent. The question is can you hear it?

When I was a teenager having to make decisions about my future career, my interest lay in the field of psychology. But because I could not see a way to make the type of life and living I wanted in this area I allowed my logical mind to override the intuitive feelings that were trying to guide me. As a result I went on a completely different path; this led me to the material rewards I was seeking but detached me from the pull of my intuition and I always felt I was doing the wrong work.

Now, many years later, I have finally followed those intuitive feelings and for the first time in my working life am doing something I truly love.

When you have a natural talent that you work on to become a master exponent and manage to earn your living doing what you love, the world seems a wonderful place. But the majority of people do not have that experience.

Those who have been lucky enough to know their area of potential, and have the resources to develop that potential, may have a headstart, but it is never too late to find your passion. But remember the law of gestation: every new project takes its own time to reach maturity.

Contra-signs:

- Lack of self-belief
- Lack of vision
- Blame mentality
- Fear of success

Exercise

Think about what you enjoy most (and least) about your job.

What are you passionate about?

How could you incorporate your passions into your career or your leisure time?

The law of purpose

A story I love, but which is probably apocryphal, illustrates this law.

Reportedly during a visit to the NASA space centre in 1962, President John F Kennedy noticed a janitor carrying a broom. He interrupted his tour, walked over to the man and said, 'Hi, I'm Jack Kennedy. What are you doing?'

'Well, Mr President,' the janitor responded, 'I'm helping put a man on the moon.'

This illustrates the concept of purpose perfectly.

Your purpose is your sense of 'why'. It is the driving inner motivation that gets you up in the morning when you would rather stay in bed, and keeps you going on the treadmill when you feel fit to drop. We feel its absence just as surely as we feel its presence. When it's not with us, our actions take huge amounts of willpower and quite often we fail as a result.

Roy F Baumeister in his book *Willpower* helps us to see that willpower is a scarce resource, easily used up and hard to renew, which is why if we rely on willpower alone to try and achieve our goals we are likely to fail.

Think of a time you wanted to lose weight, or get fit, or learn a new language, or study for that additional professional qualification. Without a sense of purpose and a deep connection to your why, your only source of power to help you achieve your goal was your willpower. If you were relying solely on willpower, then the chances are that you didn't make it to your finishing line.

A great example of this are the men and women who when they set their wedding date suddenly find the willpower to lose the weight they had been trying to lose for years. Suddenly they have a purpose and can attach their goal to their purpose and achieve their ambition. But for many, after their big day, they go back to their old ways and then wonder why some years later the wedding outfit doesn't fit.

It is your sense of purpose that really drives you.

Contra-signs:

- Life feels meaningless
- Detachment and disengagement from work and other aspects of life
- Low levels of motivation and drive
- Lack of commitment

Exercise
When did you last try and attempt a new project using mainly willpower?
What goal do you feel a sense of purpose for now?

The law of relativity

The way you view the world is governed by your perspective. Your mind is constantly balancing the issues you face and the challenges you have by prioritising them in your mind. Albert Einstein captured the essence of the law of relativity for us normal thinkers: 'Put your hand on a hot stove for a minute, and it seems like an hour. Sit with a pretty girl for an hour, and it seems like a minute. That's relativity.'

The law of relativity helps us keep a perspective on our triumphs and disasters. There will always be someone richer than you and poorer than you.

Viktor Frankl said that our freedom lies in our ability to choose our thoughts, and this is what the law of relativity allows us to do every day.

The first two lines of Kipling's classic poem 'If' sums up the importance of relativity:

'If you can keep your head when all about you/Are losing theirs and blaming it on you.'

Contra-signs:
- Lack of perspective and/or judgement
- Small issues may be viewed as big problems
- Big problems may not be dealt with until they become unmanageable
- Inability to prioritise effectively

Exercise
What would help you to gain a different perspective on the challenges you face?
If your habitual thoughts changed, would you feel different?

The law of rhythm

The universe is full of natural rhythms.

The earth rotates at the same speed every day, which we have designated to be 24 hours in duration, and as a consequence we get a sunrise and a sunset once a day. It takes 365.25 days for Earth go round the sun, and as a consequence we have seasons and the moon orbits the Earth so the tides come in and go out every day.

Women have monthly cycles. Some believe there are other biorhythms with a 23-day physical cycle, a 28-day emotional cycle and a 33-day intellectual cycle. This has never been proved scientifically but it has resonance for many people because we can feel ourselves ebb and flow. We don't always feel our best and we have good days and bad days.

The law of rhythm is all about energy. If you expend your energy trying to overcome natural rhythms, you will inevitably waste your energy and fail in your endeavours. The story of King Canute trying to hold back the tide is used to illustrate this principle. It is now widely understood as a king trying to demonstrate to his courtiers that he did not have heavenly powers and that nature could not be dominated.

Western economies have been subject to boom-and-bust cycles since the 1950s. Fashions come and go in regular cycles.

There are two aspects to the law of rhythm: not trying to fight the rhythm, and aligning your efforts and energy to take advantage of the wave that rhythm creates.

George Harrison captured the spirit of this law in his song 'All Things Must Pass'. It can be difficult to believe that, when you are in the middle of a crisis, there will be salvation around the corner. Some people get so bound up in their own publicity that they lose sight of the opposite aspect of rhythm: that life is all about change, and that success, having come, can also eventually go.

The Satir Change Curve (page 115) applies here as well. In not understanding the law of rhythm, people may give up after investing their time and money in a venture or a dream, not realising that they are actually on the verge of breaking through (the law of gestation).

We would do well to heed Kipling's message from 'If':

'If you can meet with triumph and disaster and treat those two impostors just the same'.

Contra-signs:

- Your life feels like a disaster with no end in sight
- You're on the crest of a wave and feel invincible
- Everyone else's life is a bed of roses compared to yours
- You have the sense there are forces at play that you can't overcome

---

Exercise

Keep a diary to note how your energy levels fluctuate over the course of a month.

Take steps to ensure that you are eating, sleeping and exercising appropriately during your low-energy days.

The law of perpetual transmutation of energy

Transmutation is the changing of a substance from one form into another. It is a subject that has fascinated the human mind for as long as there is recorded history, with stories of men transmuting into gods and demons, and chemists searching for the method to turn lead into gold. One of the miracles of Jesus was to turn water into wine.

It was Einstein who saw the relationship, scientifically, between energy and matter. There can be few people who are unaware of his famous equation $E=MC^2$. There is a connection between this scientific equation, the way our brains work and the way we create results in our physical world.

An idea or a thought is energy generated inside your brain. FMRI (Functional Magnetic Resonance Imaging) machines record the brain's electrical activity, so we know that a thought is carried in the brain by micro-electrical impulses. When Mozart had the ideas for all of his symphonies and sonatas, they were just electrical pulses flashing through his brain. For them to be written down he had to remember the musical thoughts for long enough so that he could put them on paper. The minute that he had written his musical thoughts down, he transmuted them from the energy of thought to the ink and paper. His thoughts had become a physical thing.

We are the only species that does this and we have been doing it for so long that we take it for granted. Every step of humankind's progress from cave dweller to builder of 100-storey skyscrapers and conqueror of the moon has been the result of the process of transmutation of thought to thing.

This process of transmutation happens at the conscious and unconscious level. At the unconscious level it is the way in which our unconscious thoughts are communicated to others through our body language of unconscious gestures, facial expressions and tone of voice. Your unconscious thoughts are turned into reality through your body. It is an irrepressible process.

Conscious success comes from understanding this process and turning it to your advantage.

Like the law of growth and decay, it can work in the positive or the negative. It will transmute positive thoughts into positive things and negative thoughts into negative things.

Reaching our potential and achieving our success in life comes from our ability to turn our thoughts into things. A thought that remains a thought has no value to anyone, not even to the thinker of the thought. It only becomes valuable when it has been turned into a thing.

If you are thinking there are thoughts that are not turned into things, take the example of the love of one person for another. If it is enduring love, then it has most definitely turned into things: into photographs that capture shared moments, love letters, texts and emails, mementos such as party invitations, not to mention a marriage contract, living in a home together or having children.

You will remember from the chapter on needs that we have an inherent need to create, to turn our thoughts into things. Whenever I run a workshop about creativity and ask delegates to come up with names of creative people, invariably the big names crop up: Michelangelo, Leonardo da Vinci, Van Gogh, Beethoven, The Beatles, Shakespeare.

The word creative has come to mean artistic in many peoples' minds because they can see the link between turning thoughts into things most easily in the work of artists, composers and authors. But this process is what lies behind everything we do. This is why cars, houses and holidays and other material goods such as watches and clothes have become so important in our lives. They represent the way in which people who are not artists, authors or composers can show how good they are at turning thoughts into things. They just do it through the medium of money. They turn their thoughts into money, which they exchange for the things they want. This is the law of perpetual transmutation of energy in action.

When you are not intuitively connected to your creativity, frustration, lack of meaning, lack of purpose and a sense of unworthiness are the natural consequences. You do not have to aspire to be the next Beatles, Mozart or Shakespeare. You have your own connection to the life force that is creation and your purpose and meaning is discovered when you give it the opportunity for full expression.

So the next question becomes, how do you give full expression to your creativity?

The answer lies in understanding the application of Einstein's equation: $E=MC^2$ to the transmutation of a thought to a thing. A thought is a combination of imagination and intelligence.

I hope that what you have read by now has convinced you that intelligence is a much broader concept than you were ever taught at school.

The perpetual transmutation of energy works at the galactic level, and can be seen in the formation and ultimate death of stars. It can be seen at the molecular level in the transformation of inert chemicals into living tissue through the organising process which is the life force, and it can be seen at work in the mind of humankind in the manifestation of things from thoughts.

In short, it takes a lot of thought, imagination and intelligence to manifest a thing.

We are led to believe that the manifestation from thoughts into things only happens for people who have big imaginations and big intelligence, and we compare ourselves on some arbitrary scale of what imagination and intelligence looks like and decide that we do not have enough.

Henry Ford had insight into this issue when he said: 'Thinking is the hardest work there is, which is probably the reason so few engage in it.'

What he meant was that when most people understand how much mental energy it takes to turn an idea into its physical manifestation, they give up because they believe it is beyond them.

But we all have imagination, we can all imagine a future that is different to today: we call this dreaming. We are all driven by our dreams, either consciously or unconsciously. Our ability to turn our dreams into reality lies in our ability to generate enough energy from our intelligence and imagination to manifest the idea into its physical reality.

There has never been anyone in history who made a dream come true without engaging and working with the intelligence of others. For example:

- Steve Jobs had semi-conductor pioneer Andy Grove as a mentor in his early days at Apple.
- Bill Gates created Microsoft with his business partner Paul Allen.
- Nikola Tesla is now regarded by many as a more influential inventor than Edison, but it was only from his collaboration with George Westinghouse that his ideas were realised for public use.
- The Beatles were just another band trying to hit the big time until they met George Martin and he helped to create the sound that would conquer the world.

To summarise: to bring about the manifestation of your thoughts into things, you have to supply sufficient imagination powered by sufficient intelligence. Imagination is a skill you can develop with the proper teaching and practice. You were born with all the intelligence you need to gather the energy necessary to turn your thoughts into things. What you weren't born with was the knowledge of how to apply your imagination and your intelligence in combination with the intelligence of others to enable your thoughts to manifest as things.

A key skill that must be developed is the ability to understand people, and through that understanding, to be able to recognise those who you can work with to manifest your thoughts into things.

Thomas Edison said: 'Opportunity is missed by most people because it is dressed in overalls and looks like work.'

Transmuting your thoughts into things is hard work and this is what separates the successful from the unsuccessful.

Contra-signs:

- Lack of faith, self-belief
- Disconnection from resourcefulness
- Cynicism
- A belief in the inability to turn thought into things leads to a negative mindset.

The law of vibration

The idea of vibration has a long history in spiritual thinking and teaching. In his book *Power vs Force*, Dr David Hawkins attempted to quantify the different levels of human energetic vibration through an experimental method borrowed from the practice of applied kinesiology. While his work has largely been discredited from a scientific perspective, I have included it here because it intuitively feels right to me, and has been very useful in helping me and my clients to understand their emotions and the physical feelings that emanate from them.

Hawkins identified seventeen vibrational frequency levels with different emotional states.

In Hawkins' model the energy of shame represents the lowest energetic vibration and enlightenment the highest.

There have been times when I have felt deep levels of shame because of things I have done or indeed not done. And I can vividly remember the drained feeling that came with that emotional state of shame. I can also remember times when I had brought forth my courage, and the feeling of energy and empowerment that came with that.

One of Hawkins' propositions is that the only way you can get yourself out of a low energetic level is by engaging your level of courage, which sits in the centre of his list of energies. This might sound like an obvious statement and it is very much how parents talk to their young children. You might recall being prompted to be a brave boy or girl or you might have encouraged your children to do the same. This is a direct call to engage your courage so that you will rise above your low emotional state. By the teenage years, we are expected to be able to control our emotions and act in a more adult fashion, but few of us have received instruction on how to do it effectively. Most adults I've met do not always know how to manage their own emotions!

So how do you raise your vibrational level? If you are in a negative state of mind – angry, sad, defeated, guilty – the only long-term way out is to raise your energetic level to courage. First, ask yourself why you feel the way you do. Your unconscious mind will give you the answer, but you have to be open to accept and receive it. This is where your courage comes in: you need courage to allow the reason for the negativity come to the surface, and you have to have a strategy to neutralise the negativity.

This is the strategy that I have used:

1. You have to adopt a growth mindset. This fills you with a desire to learn and to move away from a fixed mindset where you feel you know everything already.
2. You have to see the opportunity in every situation. The simple way to do this is to ask yourself:
   a. What can I learn from this situation?
   b. What have I learned about myself as a result of this experience?
   c. How does this experience help me grow?
3. Develop an attitude of gratitude. You will experience successes and failures and have positive and negative experiences all your life; this is inevitable. The brain's natural response to anything negative is to see it as a threat. This is the brain's evolved way of keeping you safe, therefore it will stimulate your threat reactions of fight, flight or freeze. When you develop an attitude of gratitude for the

negative experiences, you begin to turn off your brain's natural threat reaction. To help you develop gratitude for negative experiences, go back to step two and study it until you really get its significance.

The more I allowed the law of vibration to sit within me, the more sensitive I became to the energetic states of other people. This enabled me to become a far more effective communicator.

At a recent management training workshop for an international company one of the senior executives (let's call her Anne) asked to speak to myself and my colleague privately. Anne was having trouble with her boss. An intimidating man in stature and manner, he was causing her to be depressed about her job and this was affecting her life at home with her husband and daughter. She needed advice and asked to have a meeting with myself and my colleague. He and I are very different people; his approach in the conversation was to talk about some practical steps that she could take to help her. But I sensed from the energy she was projecting that this wasn't what she wanted so I talked to her about things she could do from an energetic perspective. These included defining her personal vision and thinking about how she wanted to be seen by her boss.

The next day she approached me separately and asked if she could work with me privately to help develop the aspects of thinking I had introduced her to.

The more workshops I ran the more I began to notice not just the energy of the individuals in the room but the energy of the room itself, and it became very clear to me that energetic states are contagious. Accomplished public speakers, performers, comedians are quick to recognise any change in audience mood and are able to adapt to 'win' the audience back.

As the fog of my old programming continued to lift, the old saying 'Birds of a feather flock together' came to mind. People of the same energetic state (for example, a higher positive energetic state) attract each other, and the opposite is also true, as people of widely different vibration tend to repel each other. It is only at the energetic state of love that the repulsion between the positive and negative states goes away. I do not mean sexual love. I am referring to the state where tolerance, compassion and care come to the fore, and we are no longer susceptible to others' energetic states.

I realise that the idea of energetic thinking can seem a bit 'out there', and I used to think the same until I stopped resisting the idea. This correlates to Hawkins' vibrational level of acceptance. You can only learn the lessons of any experience, positive or negative, if you have fully accepted it.

We communicate our energetic levels constantly and unconsciously through our body language. We are naturally sensitive to and very good readers of these signals. You will be able to identify people in your life who are of low or high energy.

Vibrational level must not be confused with emotional state. Vibration is a consistent state of being which guides the way in which life unfolds over time. It can be broadly divided into the positive and negative, with the vibration level of courage being the dividing point between the two. Vibration can be thought of as a long-term mental state, which is hard-wired and can be difficult to move without help and training.

Emotional states are rapid and transient. They come and go and are not connected to vibration. It is possible for someone of low or negative vibration to still experience the emotions of joy and happiness; and it is possible for someone of a high or positive vibration to experience the emotions of anger and fear, for example.

The difference between someone of high and someone of low vibration is how they deal with and manage their emotional state.

Our energetic level also effects how empathetic we feel towards to someone.

Hawkins proposes the idea that the energy of pride and desire are negative, and this took a while to sink in. I had always been taught to have pride in myself and take pride in my work. How could these very worthy sentiments be a negative force?

This is where it becomes important to recognise the difference between the inner and outer. When pride is coming from within it can be a very positive motivating force, but when pride is just a reflection of the judgement of others and your attempts to curry favour with them, it becomes a negative force.

It may seem odd that desire can be considered to be a negative vibration. This is because it is to do with the object of our desire. When we become attached to achieving our desires, whether it is a physical thing such as a car, a house or a holiday or an emotional thing such as the love of a particular person or the respect of a boss, we can lose sight of what is important and become fixated on achievement. This is what results in the 'I'll be happy when...' mentality, which as we saw on page 112 is never achievable. (the law of detachment).

You can see this play out in the myriads of people who followed career paths that other people, rather than they themselves, thought they should. It is a one-way street to a lack of fulfilment and it is rooted in the negative energies of pride and fear.

When you become conscious of your own vibrational level, you become aware of why people want to deal with you. It has nothing to do with whether you are a nice or nasty person. We are most comfortable with those whom we feel are at a similar energy or vibrational level.

Your vibrational level is the expression of your energetic state and we are very sensitive to these states and pick them up at the unconscious level so we know, without knowing how we know, when someone is faking it.

Contra-signs:

- You don't understand why people do or don't want to associate with you
- You think some people take undue risks
- You think some people are too set in their ways
- You lack confidence in yourself

Exercise

Take a challenging situation that you have experienced recently. Ask yourself:

    a. What was my emotional state?

    b. Did my emotional state change as the situation developed?

    c. What can I learn from this experience?

    d. What have I learned about my level of vibration as a result of this experience?

    e. How does this experience help me grow?

But not the law of attraction

The law of attraction has a long history in the self-development world and it was frequently referenced in one of the most influential books written about personal success, *Think and Grow Rich* by Napoleon Hill. The basic concept is that 'like attracts like'; that our thoughts are energy and if we focus on visualising positive thoughts, we are more likely to attract positive experiences and positive people. If we focus on the abundance that we already have in our lives, so the thinking goes, then this abundance will multiply.

There are many people who have attributed their success to the law of attraction. The most notable of these is Oprah Winfrey, whose rags-to-riches story is the stuff of dreams. But there are also many who have tried the principles but not achieved success.

For me the law of attraction is a combined version of some of the natural laws listed here. For me the law of attraction does not stand on its own and I have therefore not listed it as a unique natural law.

Allowing the natural laws to work for you

The natural laws are playing their part just as certainly as gravity holds you firmly to the Earth's surface. All you have to do is raise your conscious awareness of them and accept the idea that you can start working with them.

If you are having difficulty accepting the idea of natural law it is probably because you have been fed a diet of misinformation from two different angles:

First is the idea that your success in life is a consequence of how hard you work. Success is related to hard work, but only when it is applied in the right way. There are billions of people around the world who work hard but do not experience the success they want in their lives. (For clarity: I am not defining success as just the accumulation of money. Success is what you define it to be.) *Hard work is absolutely necessary for success to emerge but it has to be applied to the right actions, at the right time, in the right way.* It is the lack of connection between hard work and natural law that leads to the entitled mindset.

Second is the idea, from the spiritualist movement, that you only have to think good thoughts and chant positive mantras for the universe to provide you with what you want. As with the idea of hard work, success is related to thinking good thoughts, and mantras can help in embedding these thoughts, but they have to be applied in the right way at the right time and with the right actions or they account for nothing.

We saw in the chapter about needs that certainty is a key aspect of our core human need for security. History shows us that those who achieved their success stepped out of their comfort zone and were able to embrace the uncertainty inherent in trying new experiences, and therefore allow their natural inclination to creativity and growth its full expression.

Understanding The Journey

'Do not go where the path may lead, go instead where there is no path and leave a trail.'

Ralph Waldo Emerson

Human history is the story of evolution.

Homo sapiens was just one of many human species when it emerged around 200,000 years ago, and by about 12,000 years ago (around 10,000 BC) it had wiped out the other species to become the sole surviving human representative on earth.

The human species we are today has taken just 12,000 years to go from living in caves to developing the technology to create the modern world and to explore the solar system and beyond.

It takes approximately eighteen years for the human body to reach physical maturity, but the jury is still out as to how long it takes us to reach mental maturity.

Developments in scientific research enabled scientists to identify a turning point in human biology, when we go from physical growth to maturity and then pass into physical decline and progress towards death. Recently, and contrary to received wisdom, it has been discovered that there is a part of the brain that continually develops new cells. Jonas Frisén from the Karolinska Institutet has estimated that we produce 700 new neurons – cells that transmit information – per day in the hippocampus, the centre of emotion, memory and the autonomic nervous system. Neuroscientific research has shown us that the brain continually creates new synaptic connections and breaks existing connections. So if our brains possess this natural plasticity, why should our intelligence and personalities be fixed and limited? We are all born with the ability to learn, and isn't learning about change?

If you have a growth mindset does that give you the ability to develop your intelligence and your personality? Doesn't this question lie at the heart of every individual's right to life, liberty and the pursuit of happiness?

In a world that is always evolving it is not possible to stand still.

Einstein's great insight was that there is no fixed frame of reference in the universe. Everything is moving relative to everything else. Imagine you are driving a car at 30 mph, when a car goes past you doing 100 mph. As it goes past the sound of the engine changes as the Doppler effect squashes and then expands the soundwaves, and within a few seconds the car becomes smaller in your vision and is out of sight. We know that the other car has not physically changed but relatively it has.

This principle is at work constantly in our lives. If you rely on the thirty-two-volume printed version of the *Encyclopaedia Britannica*, you are going to be travelling at 30 mph compared to the person using Google, Wikipedia and TED. Soon you will be out of sight and irrelevant to those speeding past you.

This is the journey that mankind has been on since Homo sapiens emerged to become the only representative of humankind on the planet.

Understanding your journey is one of the four cornerstones of personal growth along with understanding your needs, understanding your resourcefulness and understanding your wisdom. It is your journey that represents the dynamic aspect of your life, without which there would be no change or growth.

The hero's journey

Joseph Campbell was a professor of the liberal arts in the US and studied mythology. His studies led to the concept of the hero's journey in his famous book *The Hero with a Thousand Faces*. It is the idea that the myths and legends of all cultures and religions can be explained by a single story structure, the monomyth.

His ideas have been adopted by many writers and thinkers, and I have found his concept a very useful vehicle in understanding my personal journey and the journey we all make through life. Mythological tales are about human experience and emerged as a way of passing on life's lessons between the generations. As we all face the same challenges in life, wherever we were born on the planet, it is not unreasonable for people to describe the journey from birth to death in similar ways.

Campbell's original hero's journey had seventeen stages. This process was later summarised into twelve stages by Hollywood executive Christopher Vogler in a Disney studio memo (in his own influential book *The Writer's Journey: mythic structure for writers*). Roughly speaking, these stages are:

1. The call to adventure
2. Refusal of the call
3. The appearance of the guide
4. Crossing the threshold into the special world
5. The trials
6. Face your demons
7. The ultimate challenge
8. Crisis: return to status quo or adopt new identity
9. Emerge from the struggle
10. Return to the old world
11. Resolution
12. New status quo: higher level.

The call to adventure

The call to adventure is a metaphor for a new challenge in your life. This is represented in myths, stories and modern films, from *The Wizard of Oz* to *Star Wars* to *The Lord of The Rings*.

We tend to think of the call to adventure as the big events in life, for example:

- The first day at school
- Moving from junior school to high school
- From high school to university
- From university to work
- From single life to married life
- From independence to parenthood.

These landmarks are easily recognised, but it is the less obvious calls to adventure that arise throughout our lives that we are more likely to resist. For instance, your parent is diagnosed with Alzheimer's disease and you feel the call to support him or her. A common call is the lure of self-employment. It may be the realisation that a marriage isn't working any more. You might be aware of an injustice that needs to be addressed and feel the call to do something about it. Politicians can become motivated to campaign for new laws when they witness acts of inhumanity. Whether it is the offer of a promotion or a new relationship, it is your perception of the risk involved that determines how likely you are to accept the call.

A call to adventure often manifests itself as a difficulty that needs resolving. In films there may be someone to help reveal the call, but in real life you very often have to recognise and respond to the call yourself.

Refusal of the call

We often see this in movies, when the central character hovers on the brink of a new challenge, reluctant to take it on. It might come in the form of the offer of new job, the need to support an ill parent or maybe the feeling that you want to start a charity. The call can come from any direction and appear in many ways.

The reality for many people is that they do not even recognise the call when it comes. Because it doesn't always come gift wrapped as a golden opportunity and presented to you. It might appear as a nagging feeling that something isn't right and that you need to make a change. It can appear as a suggestion from a friend that falls outside your comfort zone. But of course it can be a very clear opportunity. You are offered a promotion at work but feel it is outside your capabilities and your mind is telling you, you don't want the added responsibility. Or it might be the opportunity to join a friend in a new business venture and in that moment you start to wonder if you can really trust your friend or whether you want to give up your safe and secure job.

The appearance of the guide

In *Star Wars*, Luke Skywalker receives a holographic recorded distress message. Not understanding the message he seeks out the help of an old sage who lives in the hills, Obi-Wan Kenobi. In real life we rarely have an obvious guide or a mentor like Obi-Wan Kenobi, or Gandalf in *The Lord of The Rings*, or Dumbledore in the *Harry Potter* films.

This part can very often be missing in real life. So what we tend to do is to go and seek out a guide for advice and counsel. Of course we approach people we trust and here is the inherent problem for most.

In the idealised version of the journey The Guide is always someone who will challenge you to go beyond your existing boundaries and self-belief, but, when we seek out our own guide we tend to go to those who will support us in the choices we make but who will rarely challenge us to break out of our mould.

This is one reason why the coaching industry is seeing such explosive growth. There is an increasing understanding that to break out of your existing patterns you need someone to challenge you to do so.

Crossing the threshold into the special world

Crossing the threshold represents the breaking from the old ties and the leap into the dark of the new aspect of your life. Watch out for this in movies when the main character enters a new arena (literally in *The Hunger Games*, or when Billy Elliot starts ballet classes). This is usually marked by a mixture of feelings: of excitement, fear and uncertainty, but it is marked with a sense of purpose.

This can be a stumbling point in real life when the unfamiliarity of the new, coupled with the challenge, can lead you to question whether you made the right choice.

The trials

As soon as you start on your journey the trials start. These are the tests that take you outside of your comfort zone. The trials require you to learn new skills and push yourself beyond what you thought was possible. This is the point where you start to encounter the limiting beliefs you hold about yourself and become acutely aware of your self-image.

For many people this represents the exciting part of life. Being tested to learn more and improve existing skills can be seen as energising and dynamic, but for many others it is a time of fear as they worry about their ability to cope and to learn.

Age can often be seen as a barrier to personal development for some people. But pace of technological change nowadays and the fact that people are living longer means the opportunity to carry on learning and growing is there for everyone who chooses it. However, the freedom that existed when change took place at a much slower pace, not to grow and to ignore the trials of life is less of an option than in years gone by.

Face your demons

We all have demons. They stem from our beliefs about the things we think we can't do and what we believe to be true about the world.

When the Spanish, led by Hernán Cortés, were conquering the new world of South America in the sixteenth century it is said that his soldiers were frightened of the tribes they were to encounter. So Cortés instructed his lieutenants to burn the boats on which they arrived to ensure that his men had no option but to face their fears and were motivated to fight to survive.

Some people are so afraid of facing their demons that they withdraw from the world, but the rest of us tend to make trade-offs, deciding which demons we're prepared to face and which are just too much to contemplate. For example, we might decide that we're no good at small talk and so go out of our way to avoid a networking event that might have led to a new opportunity.

The problem comes when our demons get in the way of us leading the life we want to lead. If your dream is to be a doctor, then a fear of public speaking and performing is not going to hold you back. But if you want to be a surgeon, fearing the sight of blood and gore probably will.

When our fears are clear-cut they can influence us to choose a different path in life and to put childhood ambitions and dreams into the attics of our mind. The trouble is that dreams never go away and we are always left wondering what might have been… if only we'd had the courage to follow our dream.

If you are going to accept your call to adventure and the challenges that come with it, you will inevitably be called to face your demons.

The ultimate challenge

The ultimate challenge is easily recognised in action films. In *Star Wars* it is to blow up the Death Star, in *The Lord of The Rings* to destroy the ring, in *The Wizard of Oz* to defeat the wicked witch. In real life the ultimate challenge might be a personal goal to lose weight, stop drinking or taking on a new role or project. The ultimate challenge can exist in different aspects of our lives, personal, with our family or friends, and in our professional lives. For many the ultimate challenge is how to make a demanding professional life work successfully with a happy family life.

Crisis: return to status quo or adopt new identity

Ancient Chinese philosopher Lao Tzu said that in order to become who we might be, we have to let go of who we are.

This is a key stage in your journey and is the point at which many people don't want to progress. We've invested a lot in becoming who we are. Who we are represents our lifetime of experiences and learning. Our identity is a marker for everyone who knows us. But one of the biggest barriers to letting go of who you are can be the people in your life who are comfortable with who you are right now. You might see this in friends and colleagues who don't support you in the changes you want to make because of the uncertainty it raises within them. It can get in the way of people who want to take up a new hobby, stop drinking or give up smoking because their friends put them under pressure to maintain their old habits so they don't feel threatened.

I saw this force at work when I worked for a short time with a charity that supported young offenders. The biggest problem the young men faced was going back to their old communities which had been part of the reason they had ended up in prison. The old friends had a vested interest in not allowing the newly released friend to start afresh. Even with the support of the charity some were unable to stay out of trouble and ended up back in jail.

At work we see this force at play in managers who pigeonhole the people in their teams based on their perceptions of that person. It was only as I recognised the significance of the hero's journey that I realised I was also guilty of this pigeonholing. Once someone has created an identity for themselves in the workplace that is not serving them on their journey, it becomes very difficult for them to allow their full potential to be developed, as those in power take away the opportunities to continue the journey within that organisation. Very often the only option is to start afresh elsewhere and literally reinvent yourself. You might recognise this as the call to adventure and the start of another journey.

For many the thought of losing friendships and relationships and facing up to their fears is too daunting, and they reject their call to adventure and stay locked in a life that is unfulfilling. This leads to the belief that there is nothing you can do to change your circumstances. In the worst case it leads to long-term frustration and even despair as you sense what you could have achieved if only you had been brave enough to take the chance.

For those who do accept the challenge and come through the identity crisis, a new life of opportunity awaits. This phase brings feelings of excitement and empowerment born from overcoming the internal struggle. But along with those feelings comes the uncertainty of a future yet to be shaped.

Emerge from the struggle

In the world of myth and movies, as the hero emerges from the struggle he might be rewarded with a new kingdom, the hand of the prince or princess, or to give this symbolic reward another name, 'the Holy Grail'. In modern terms this might be a promotion at work, the hand of your loved one or the path that opens up ahead.

The reward can be physical or it can be the opportunity to start a new life with the new power you have gained by taking on and overcoming your demons.

Entering this stage feels like you have become a new person. Stronger for your struggles so far but aware that there are further challenges ahead. The call of the old life is still strong at this point and you can see it at play in the real world in people who embark on training courses but never implement their learning to move forward.

Return to the old world

This is the idea of the return of the conquering hero. Having gone off to face the challenges the hero returns to their old country to acclaim and recognition. This is where reality bites. In films the hero returns to a rapturous welcome, but this may not be the case in real life.

When Microsoft had become one of the world's biggest and most powerful organisations Bill Gates was not seen as a hero by everyone; some saw him as a megalomaniac out to control the world. If you take on your hero journey because of the plaudits you want to receive as a returning hero, you are likely to be disappointed. You must take on your journey purely for your own reasons and with successful completion of the journey as your only objective.

When you come through your journey you will be changed in some way, and you will have conquered fears, developed new skills and taken on challenges that will have helped you grow into a more aware person than you were before. Life will not be the same. This will be marked by having new people in your life who resonate with you at your new level of awareness.

Resolution

This is the last part of the journey and represents your own unconditional acceptance of yourself as you really are. Your identity is no longer shaped by anyone except yourself and you willingly take full responsibility for how you appear in the world.

This is the level of true independence. You are not dependent on anyone else for approval, for love, for status. At this level you are in harmony with your creativity and know how to give it to the world.

New status quo: higher level

You are at a new level ready to start another journey. But now the journey can be one of your choice rather than one of external calling. We see examples of many sportspeople who reach their peak and never seem to perform at those levels again. This marks the start of a new journey, with new challenges and tests to be faced – for example, tennis champion Andre Agassi achieved greatness then fell away, made an astounding comeback and then as his tennis career faded set up a school for disadvantaged kids.

You are on this journey whether you like it or not

You may not be consciously aware of the journey and the stages of which it is made up or that you may have already been on this path. We can tend to think of the journey as only being relevant to high-profile people, such as sports, film and pop stars, and can find it harder to relate it to ourselves because we do not see ourselves as heroes.

But you are a hero and you are on your journey.

Why we don't understand the importance of the journey

I wish I had known someone who could have helped me understand the journey, and the role it has in shaping the decisions we make, earlier in my life, but maybe I just wasn't ready to listen.

You are always on a journey, whatever your walk of life and whatever stage of life you are at. Whether you are at the start of your life or coming to the end you are always on a journey with potential to receive a new call to adventure

The idea of the journey is a very powerful framework around which you can build and sustain a way of understanding life's trials and tribulations. This will help you to recognise life's challenges for what they are: your call to grow into the person that you have the potential to be.

What gets in the way of understanding the journey?

Although we are not specifically taught about the journey we are taught to prioritise the destination, whatever it is. This is usually the goal of passing an exam or getting a job or going to university. This means we are always living in the future.

When your focus is the destination it leads to a sense of lacking and is recognisable by feelings such as: 'I'll be happy when…' I get that promotion/ fall in love/get married/have children/buy that new car etc. Or it might be 'I'll be able to relax when…' or 'I'll be able to enjoy myself when…'

These are all signs that you don't understand the flow of the journey.

The journey is rarely revealed to us in detail. If you are employed in a big organisation you might have a career mapped out and therefore some sense of what your journey looks like. But increasingly that long-term view is not there for most. Businesses are restructuring regularly to accommodate changes in technology and new competitors that change the commercial landscape.

If you are an entrepreneur or business owner you are likely to be more familiar with a shorter time frame and the fact that unexpected things are going to happen that you have to adapt to or face the consequences.

However, there is one way in which you can become more aware of your real journey, and that is by becoming more consciously aware of your emotional state and in particular your emotional reaction to new challenges.

EXERCISE

Over the next week keep a diary of times you felt emotions such as stress, anxiety or fear and note what brought on these feelings. You might call these feelings the emotional markers of your journey, and the first step to becoming aware of your journey is becoming aware of these markers.

One of the common complaints of employers I have met is that people come to them with a sense of entitlement. This might be in the form of a good salary, responsibility or status, but it is borne from the idea they have been infused with from an early age: that they are working towards a final destination. By the age of twenty-one/twenty-two many university graduates view their degree as a ticket to the career club, and they expect to be rewarded, but the reality is they have just started a new phase of their journey.

A growth mindset equips you with the tools you need to take on the journey. *You will need curiosity, flexibility, patience and endurance.* When you have a fixed mindset you will only get so far before you become frustrated by the natural obstacles you will meet along the way.

The emotionally intelligent journey

In a real journey, you travel through scenery. It might be green rolling hills, high rugged mountains, stark city skylines or dry desert flats, but you experience highs and lows in terms of the sensual stimuli of sight, sound, smell and hearing. For me, the smell of the sea and the feel of the sea breeze is one of the most energising sensual experiences.

In the journey through life, your emotions are like the marker posts of the tests and challenges you face. Your emotional intelligence is the instrument that allows you to read the markers accurately. This journey is about personal growth, and your ability to navigate it successfully is a consequence of your emotional mastery.

The idea of emotional intelligence was brought into the popular domain by Daniel Goleman in his book *Emotional Intelligence: why it can matter more than IQ*. The four cornerstones of Goleman's model of emotional intelligence are:

1. Self-awareness
2. Self-management

3. Awareness of others
4. Relationship management.

Understanding your journey is a way of recognising the need to master these four skills.

• Self-awareness

Emotional mastery is not about trying to control or eliminate your emotions. We have a word for people with no emotion – psychopaths. Our emotions are integral parts of us and the way in which we form relationships, and without them we have no connection with other people.

Emotional mastery is being able to recognise that you are in an emotional state, awareness of what level that state is (high, medium or low), and whether that state is serving you.

It is important to recognise the difference between emotional mastery and emotional denial. Many people will deny their emotional response to events as a mechanism to cope. But emotions do not go away. They linger and they become stronger. Left unacknowledged and denied, emotions are the cause of the stress response in the body and over time this can then manifest as physical illness.

Emotional mastery allows the recognition and acknowledgement of your emotions and with that recognition the ability to choose your response to the world so you are not hostage to your emotional reactions.

• Self-management

Anyone who has worked with a person who controls their emotions will recognise them as seeming cold or unapproachable. Many people in business purposefully adopt this approach as a self-protective measure: if you don't allow yourself to feel emotionally connected to the decisions you make, you can't be hurt by them. The downside is that you don't feel the joy of them either. These people are the polar opposite of their counterparts who allow themselves to be connected to their emotions, who we describe as warm-hearted.

Our emotions are created in our minds but they are communicated through our body. In a high emotional state our hearts flutter, we sweat more, our mouths get dry, our muscles tense and our facial expression changes. Emotional mastery is the development of your self-awareness so that you can recognise your state of emotional arousal and the effect it is having on your physical body. When you have developed this awareness it becomes much easier to understand other people and the emotional reactions they are experiencing.

The value of Joseph Campbell's description of the journey is that it enables you to see the points in life when your emotions are likely to be triggered, and with this greater awareness lies the ability to choose.

Auschwitz survivor Viktor Frankl described this in the most beautiful way: 'Everything can be taken from a man but one thing: the last of the human freedoms – to choose one's attitude in any given set of circumstances, to choose one's own way.'

From the moment you were born you started your journey through life. Your early experiences shaped the way you reacted to the world as you grew into adulthood and beyond. Your journey is your road to self-awareness and emotional mastery, and it is only in consciously taking the journey and rising to the challenges it presents that you achieve the human freedom Viktor Frankl talked about: the freedom to choose.

- Awareness of others

The third cornerstone of emotional intelligence is awareness of others, or empathy. As you go consciously on your journey and become aware of the trials that are triggering the emotional reactions you are experiencing, it becomes easier to understand the emotional reactions that others are experiencing on their journey.

Your journey will create conflicts, both internal and external, in your life that may seem intractable at the time. One of the signs of internal conflict is the anxiety created when your values are challenged, and they inevitably will be; this will trigger your emotions. For example, loyalty is often challenged when you have to choose between the people you know and love and a new opportunity that requires you to take a new direction. Or you may experience it from the other side, as a friend or lover makes a decision because of the journey they are on.

- Relationship management

The last cornerstone is relationship management. Anyone who experiences true and long-lasting success achieves it with the help of others. Entrepreneurs need a team of people to make their business ideas come to fruition. Musicians need arrangers and record producers, backing singers and managers. Doctors need receptionists, scientists need research assistants. No one achieves success on their own; so the ability to build, develop and maintain relationships is a key skill and it is founded in the understanding of emotional intelligence.

Life really is a journey

It is unfortunate that the description of life's journey has become somewhat of a cliché and that we are a totally results-driven society.

The principle of seeking results rather than understanding, learning from and enjoying the journey is rooted in our early upbringing, from our first days at school. Our education system teaches us that what is important is the end result and not the learning we gain along the way.

Now I know that those in charge of our education system would say that a focus on results is what enables the system to show that learning has taken place. But this is erroneous thinking at best and hugely damaging at worst, as children start to build self-images of being successes or failures, of being capable or incapable, from an early age.

This self-image gets carried through adolescence and adulthood and is only transcended by those who are lucky enough to have a natural growth mindset.

But the good news is it is never too late to develop a growth mindset.

And the really great news is that if you do choose to develop your growth mindset, a whole new world of opportunity and challenge opens up to you, and what is more you can enjoy every step of the journey, not just hold out for the end result.

POSITIVITY AND NEGATIVITY

'Try not to become a man of success. Rather become a man of value.'
Albert Einstein

When I was younger I was often encouraged to lighten up and it always used to leave me feeling flummoxed. From my point of view, I wasn't being serious, I was concentrating. Why couldn't people see the difference? And it always generated a negative response from me.

As I look back with hopefully a little more wisdom than I had in those days, I can see these interactions for what they were: a playing out of the natural laws described in the Wisdom chapter, specifically the law of action and reaction.

It is really important that you develop an understanding of the relationship between positivity and negativity. In itself it is an expression of the law of polarity. What it means is that everything that can be expressed positively can also be expressed negatively, and vice versa. An old Zen master story illustrates this idea nicely: On his fourteenth birthday a boy is given a horse, everybody in the village says, 'How wonderful. The boy got a horse', but the Zen master says, 'We'll see.' Two years later, the boy falls off the horse, breaks his leg, and everyone in the village says, 'How terrible', but the Zen master says, 'We'll see.' Then, a war breaks out and all the young men have to go off to fight, except the boy because his leg is damaged from the fall. Everybody in the village says, 'How wonderful.'

But the Zen master says, 'We'll see.'

Every situation can have a positive or negative interpretation but the real importance is your vibration. It is your vibration level that will determine which interpretation you see.

It also applies to the law of giving and receiving. What you give you get, so if you give out positivity you get positivity back. If you give negativity you receive negativity.

If you are reading this with any scepticism I urge you to think about examples from your own life. Most people who have a negative approach to life do not recognise it as such. Their perspective seems like a realistic assessment of life and those who do not share it are, in their view, wearing rose-tinted spectacles.

If the optimist wears rose-tinted specs, then the pessimist wears grey. You will always filter life through the lenses of your current beliefs about yourself and the world.

Positive psychology

I was also to discover positive psychology, popularised in 1998 by psychologist Martin Seligman. I was drawn to this because it takes the opposite view of traditional psychology, which seeks to understand why some people don't function properly within society. Instead, positive psychology studies the phenomena that make human life enjoyable. It proposes thinking strategies that enable us to get the best out of ourselves.

Seligman became the champion for positive psychology because of his earlier work, dating back to 1975, which led him to develop the theory of learned helplessness. This is the idea that when we are subject to circumstances that have a hugely negative effect on our lives we adopt the mantle of the victim, unable to change our fate or destiny.

Reading the works of Seligman, Frankl and many others in this sphere helped me to change my self-image from victim to empowered thinker and it was this quote from his work that provided the impetus: 'Everything can be taken from a man but one thing: the last of human freedoms – to choose one's attitude in any given set of circumstances, to choose one's own way.' The work of Frankl and Seligman illuminated the importance of a positive outlook and the elimination of negativity.

Negative does not attract positive

When it comes to positivity and negativity in people, like attracts like. Positive is attracted to positive and negative is attracted to negative. You may notice this in the friends that people have, in the associations they make at work and in the results they achieve in life.

We often see people together who seem to be opposites. My brother is quite a spiritual person, and he has a partner who is very driven and works in the financial industry. On the face of it they would appear to be opposites, but their attraction works at the level of the deep psyche. At this level they are alike.

Relationships fail because of differences at the level of the deep psyche. We can like people who are the polar opposite to ourselves, but if the differences are fundamental, over time the relationship will struggle to survive.

Exercise
How negative or positive are those whom you feel closest to?
As you think about this, what questions come up in your mind about your polarity. Are you positive or negative in your vibration?

Negativity and positivity together

When high levels of negativity and positivity exist together either in the same person or in a relationship, it creates disorder, inner conflict and turmoil. Positivity and negativity together do not cancel each other out.

Real success is only achieved through clarity of thought.

Some people with a strongly negative outlook can still achieve astounding results. With total negativity comes total clarity, focus and therefore the possibility of such results. There are many examples in history of highly negative people who have become successful: Adolf Hitler, Idi Amin, Pol Pot. Their negative energy attracts other negative energy and they become powerful.

However, if you accept the definition of success that includes the idea of not preventing anyone else from achieving their success, hopefully you will see that true success cannot come from a negative mindset.

Those who have both strong positive and negative mindsets find it hard to achieve great success because their conflicting mindsets prevent them from seeing clearly and taking the decisive action that is necessary to become successful.

True success only comes when negativity is eliminated, creating a positive mindset.

The brain's natural state is negative

If your computer has ever crashed you might be familiar with the instruction to start the computer in safe mode. The brain has a similar mechanism running all the time. It has evolved to become extremely sensitive to potential threats and it can perceive them at an unconscious level.

Left to its own devices the brain's natural interpretation of events, whether they are physical, mental or emotional, is in the negative.

That's why religions and spiritual teachings demand positive thinking as a regular practice either as part of prayer or meditation.

Positivity has to be practised with discipline until it becomes a habit and can force out the weeds of negativity.

Exercise
Keep a daily diary for the next two days and note every negative thought you have. In this context negative will include any feelings of frustration, irritation, anxiety, stress. Now activate your gratitude in response to these events (see page 157).

Eliminating the negative mindset

Negative people pay a high price for achieving success. It is only achievable by the maintenance of fear or the domination of their supporters. This is the modus operandi of all despots and criminal gangs but it is also alive and kicking in many businesses and organisations.

It is important to understand how success may be achieved by the negative mindset because its seed exists within all of us. The negative energies of grief, fear, lust, anger and pride can be highly energising and motivating states. It is not uncommon for people to achieve amazing things in the aftermath of negative events. For instance, parents who raise large sums for charities, motivated by the grief of losing a child, or activists who create social movements from the anger caused by injustice and suffering. In the short term, negativity can be an immensely powerful motivating force, but left unchecked, negativity can become a drain on your energy and resilience.

Over time it has to be replaced by a positive mindset that is energising for you as an individual and for the people in your life.

You have to remain vigilant for the signs of any negativity in your thinking.

The gratitude attitude

There is only one way to eliminate negativity and that is through the correct practice of gratitude, in a disciplined and regular manner. *But eliminating negativity is not the same as eliminating negative emotion.* This is the big mistake that many people make, especially those who work in the corporate world. If you try to cut off your negative emotions, you also cut off your positive emotions.

If you are a frequently angry person, as I once was, you cannot suppress your anger without having a knock-on effect on your joy and happiness. The reality is you can only suppress negative emotions and not eliminate them altogether. Emotional suppression is a technique we learn to use to manage our relationships as we grow up. It is a very necessary social skill and without it our relationships would not survive very long. From an early age we are taught to count to ten before responding if we are feeling very strong negative emotions. However, this is only effective if we are very skilful at concealing our emotional state from others. Because we are so attuned to picking up the emotional state of others from facial expressions, we can pick up the incongruity between words spoken and body language.

Emotional suppression only works when you can effectively mask your true feelings from others, but research has shown that the long-term suppression of emotions leads to stress, which can lead to physical illnesses such as heart disease and reduced immune function, resulting in higher susceptibility to disease, impaired digestive function and other physical symptoms. It may also lead to psychological problems and mental illness such as depression.

It is this understanding that is leading to the interest in emotional intelligence and the role it can play in creating, developing and maintaining relationships and mental health.

It is natural that you will feel negative emotions when something bad happens. It would be psychopathic not to have these feelings. Research in 2010 showed that psychopathy is three times more prevalent in the corporate world than other walks of life, and in his book *Recognise Your Enemy*, Dr Z Bobich identifies fourteen types of psychopathic behaviours in the workplace. The unfortunate fact is that many of these behaviours, such as lack of remorse, superficial charm and unwarranted self-worth, are actively rewarded within the working culture of many corporate organisations.

Eliminating negativity – as opposed to eliminating negative emotions – has four stages:

1. Activating your gratitude in response to events that happen in your life.
2. Learning how to explain rather than express your emotions.
3. Learning how to gain understanding from your experiences so that you can grow as a person.
4. Connecting to your true creativity so you are living in harmony with your life force.

When you truly reach this level of awareness you will be at a level not attained by many people. If you reach it from an intuitive approach to life you may find it difficult to understand why other people do not see the world in the same way that you do, and this can lead to intolerance and become a route back to negativity. I experienced this myself when people didn't share my vision of the future.

Faith over doubt

It is unfortunate that the word faith has come to be so closely associated with organised religion. This association has meant that the word is difficult for many to understand and therefore to allow into their life. In its simplest form, your faith is your willingness to trust in your natural creativity and in your life force to give you the power to manifest your creativity in the real world. Faith is your self-belief.

The fact you are alive means you have the force of life within you. This means you have a unique combination of talents and qualities and it is your natural drive to try and express your creativity in the world. Your faith, your self-belief, is simply your ability to emotionally connect to your life force and creativity and maintain it in the face of setbacks.

Confucius said: 'Our greatest glory is not in falling but in rising every time we fall.'

Richard Branson said: 'You don't learn to walk by following rules. You learn by doing, and by falling over.'

Aristotle said: 'It is possible to fail in many ways... while to succeed is possible only in one way.'

It is this ability to maintain faith and self-belief in the face of setbacks that separates those who are successful in life and those who are not. And success has a very specific meaning:

I am frequently asked: What is success? Success is living the life you want to lead on your terms. It is achieved by having a vision of what you want to achieve in life, and achieving it without stopping anyone else from achieving what they want in life.

You have to work on your faith and your self-belief. It is like a muscle. It becomes stronger with effective use and weaker if it is not exercised.

The opposite of faith is doubt

Doubt is the exact opposite of faith, and part of the brain's natural function. Doubt and negativity are kindred spirits that work hand in glove and their role is to keep you safe, but when they are not balanced by faith they will stop you dead in your tracks when it comes to reaching out and achieving your success.

You can see and feel doubt in action all around you. It shows itself in:

- procrastination
- perfectionism
- fault-finding
- aggression
- submission
- pettiness
- criticism
- moaning
- blaming

When you are thinking about your vision for the future, it will probably look different to your current life. It will trigger doubts in your mind because you don't know how you are going to get there. Because if you did know how to get there you would already have done it and be where you want to be.

There is only one antidote to doubt and that is faith. The only way to develop faith is to develop trust in your resourcefulness, which allows you to handle unfamiliar situations. People who become successful do not wait until they know how to do something before they take the first steps towards achieving their goals. It takes faith and courage to begin without knowing how your vision will come into being.

The science fiction writer Ray Bradbury said: 'You've got to jump off a cliff and build your wings on the way down.'

It is your resourcefulness that allows you to build your wings.

Doubts become beliefs

It is one of life's cruelties that the negative will happily multiply and become more powerful of its own accord, while the positive aspect has to be consciously nurtured and willed to prominence.

This is never truer than when it comes to doubts. If we are not vigilant and do not deal with doubts when they arise, they can solidify into beliefs that become very difficult to change.

Mahatma Gandhi understood this well when he said:

Your beliefs become your thoughts,
Your thoughts become your words,
Your words become your actions,
Your actions become your habits,
Your habits become your values,
Your values become your destiny.

Doubt is a corrosive emotion. It will eat away at your relationships if you allow it to grow in your mind, and it will ultimately eat away at your own sense of self.

Eliminating negativity

I hope you now have a clear picture of why there can be no place for negativity in your mind if you are going to create and achieve your vision and realise your success.

Remember, negativity is not the same as experiencing negative emotions. You will experience negative emotions on your journey to success; the key is to develop an understanding of their purpose.

I remember my very first sales job. I was given a list of names and telephone numbers and my job was to try and sell sponsorship of an exhibition. Having no previous experience of doing this and no training, before picking up the phone for the first time my emotional state was about as high as it could be.

A lot was riding on my success as I had been recommended for the job.

After half an hour of making calls no one would speak to me and I thought I must be the most useless sales person ever. I hadn't been told that the success rate in cold (where the customer doesn't know you) telephone sales calling was about 1 in every 100 calls. I'd made fifteen calls and got nothing. In my mind the only reason could be me. I went into a state of deep anxiety before every call, my hand shaking before I picked up the receiver. However, somehow I kept my positivity about the job. I had no choice really because I didn't have many other options. But it didn't take away the fear of rejection I felt before every call.

When I analysed the results some weeks later I'd achieved about 1 percent success rate. In line with the average.

If only someone had told me this statistic before I started, it would have saved a lot of emotional turmoil and self-doubt.

Dealing with negativity in others

What you will find is that as you eliminate the negativity from your mind, it becomes easier to deal with the negativity you come across in others.

When you are full of negativity, the negativity you come across in other people can be like a spark to a petrol tank. It can set you off in many different ways: you may join forces with negative people but equally you may collide with them in confrontation. Another of Carl Jung's sayings is: 'Everything that irritates us about others can lead us to an understanding of ourselves.'

In other words, what irritates us in others is a reflection of what we don't like about ourselves.

When we eliminate negativity in our mindset, this irritation passes because we have lost that reflection of ourselves. We are free to choose our response to the situation.

You should not underestimate the impact that eliminating negativity will have on your outlook. It will change the way you see yourself and the world and it will change your opinion of other people. Some you will choose to keep in your life and some relationships you will choose to move on from.

How to use The Thinking Revolution

'What's important is that you have faith in people, that they're basically good and smart, and if you give them tools, they'll do wonderful things with them.'

Steve Jobs

What I needed, when I was sitting on the floor crying into my wine, was a plan, and I didn't have one.

Every self-help programme I investigated required me to sit down and write down my goals and the ambitions I held for myself, and I couldn't. All I knew was that I didn't want to feel the way I did and that I didn't want to make the same mistakes in the years I had left. Neither did I want a well-meaning counsellor asking me how I felt, as I knew that all too well. Behavioural cognitive therapy and the thought of journaling my behaviours every day also left me cold.

What I needed was a new way of thinking that would enable me to understand myself and other people better so that I could still be me, but not allow the trials of life to pull me down as they had in the past.

In 1687 Sir Isaac Newton published the book which included his famous three laws of motion:

1. Every object in a state of uniform motion tends to remain in that state of motion unless an external force is applied to it.
2. The acceleration of an object depends on its mass and the forces acting on it.
3. For every action there is an equal and opposite reaction.

It was the discovery of natural law that helped me to turn my thinking around. And when I started to see that Newton's laws could apply equally to human beings and the course our lives take it was as if a cloak of darkness was lifted from my eyes.

Newton's laws can be restated as the three laws of human motion:

1. We will carry on in the direction we are headed (towards our unconscious goals) unless we consciously choose to apply a different force to enable us to change direction towards intentional goals.
2. The rate at which we move towards our goals is dependent on our ability to think and the forces that affect the way we think are conscious or unconscious. In the absence of conscious force, the unconscious force will exert its influence.
3. Our brain's instinctive reaction is to resist a new force in our life in case it is a threat. To overcome this resistance we have to engage our willpower.

My aim is that *The Thinking Revolution* will help you become conscious of the forces that govern the way you think so that you can purposefully choose and follow a course of your own making, to your place of intuitive success.

Along the way you will need to reconnect to and develop your resourcefulness, allow and evolve your wisdom and accept that you have natural needs that are the motivating forces that drive your actions and behaviours.

When we are born our resourcefulness only exists as potential inside us. That is the excitement of life. As new parents we look at our newborn child and wonder at the life they will have and how it will evolve. We look forward to seeing them grow and conquering the various stages of life, walking, talking, going to school. We wonder about our ability to help them through these stages and what their life journey will bring to them. (Our life journey is now also following a different path. We've been preparing for it for nine months but then we realise that nothing can prepare us for it and our lives will never be the same again.)

In the early years of life, our needs have to be fulfilled by our parents. Our path to maturity is about developing our resourcefulness so we can become self-sufficient. The baby's journey is defined solely by its determination to get its core survival needs met. Manifest resourcefulness is low and wisdom is purely instinctive.

A key part of the parental role is to help the child to develop her resourcefulness so that she doesn't have to cry to get what she wants.

The process of growing up is about developing our resourcefulness so that we can get our needs met ourselves. As we grow, so our needs grow. Our needs are driven by natural internal factors but also by the social mores of the culture in which we grow up. All societies require their children to reach a stage where they can look after themselves, become self-sufficient and contribute to their society. As we mature our needs evolve, our resourcefulness develops, our wisdom emerges and the journey we are on starts to become apparent.

When Carol Dweck described growth and fixed mindsets she was talking about the difference between those who have a natural instinct for growing their resourcefulness and having the satisfaction of successfully fulfilling their needs, and those who do not have a natural understanding of this relationship.

You will know people who moan and blame others or circumstances for the situation in which they find themselves. They may get angry when life doesn't work out as they want it to or break down in tears when they face challenges that they don't believe they can meet.

These reactions are not dissimilar to those of the baby who cries when they are hungry, dirty or tired and many adults do not significantly mature from the emotional childhood, leaving them hostage to their emotional reactions to life. But the biology of our brains means we have the potential to go through life learning and developing new skills. It is this facility of neuroplasticity that means you can decide to change your attitude at any time, and if you have the techniques to support you, you can develop your resourcefulness whenever you want. Remember, you have the potential for infinite resourcefulness.

Unconscious versus conscious learning

In our early years our learning happens unconsciously. When we have learned to talk and communicate we develop the ability to learn consciously, but we continue to learn unconsciously as well.

Each of us has a vast database of past experiences that holds immense value, if we are able to reflect on that database in a state of detachment.

The story of our life is the way in which we apply our resourcefulness to fulfil our needs within the world we know. The world we know and the lessons we learn along the way combine to create our wisdom, and our journey emerges as the road we travel as these three aspects of our life interact together.

If there is one thing that separates us as humans from the rest of the animal kingdom it is our ability to choose to do things differently. But here lies the dilemma for most people. We become educated and socialised not to use and realise the very potential we were born with; and we look on with amazement at the people who do. We idolise them as heroes but we hold back from becoming the hero of our own story.

The great writer Ralph Waldo Emerson said: 'What lies behind us and what lies before us are tiny matters compared to what lies within us.'

Recognising your resistance

We know that our modern brains have the same biological structures – amygdala, hippocampus, parietal lobes – as the brains of early humans 200,000 years ago, but we live different lives today. The majority of the world's population doesn't live in caves and we don't have to face wild animals to survive our daily lives, and yet we still experience the same emotional responses our ancestors did.

It was only when I accepted Einstein's maxim 'It is only when we accept our limitations that we move beyond them' that I started to make progress. This meant overcoming my resistance towards learning and opening myself up to concepts such as spirituality. I wasn't yet over the grief of the break-up of my marriage but I was finally at the point of fully accepting my responsibility for it. This sent me into a deeper stage of grief as I realised the poverty I had experienced in my life as a result of being so cut off from my emotions and the spiritual side of my life.

Your resourcefulness supports your needs

We apply our resourcefulness to try and fulfil our needs. When we do this ineffectively we can experience profound emotional reactions.

Imagine that you are arranging a party to mark an important occasion and you invited 150 friends, family and work colleagues to come along and celebrate with you. A hundred people accept your invitation and so you hire a venue that can cater for this number, you arrange the catering, the drinks and entertainment at considerable expense. On the night only seventy-five people show up. How do you feel now?

And how would you have felt if only thirty people had turned up?

When I asked clients these questions a range of answers emerged: frustrated, rejected, angry, concerned, to name a few. In every case they admitted they would have an emotional reaction. The level of your emotional reaction will depend on the type of person you are.

This example shows that when you are ineffective in satisfying your needs you will always experience an emotional reaction. If your experience is consistent over time this will then feed into your beliefs. You might come to believe that you are not very good at throwing parties, you might question the depth of your friendships, and how your friends value your friendship.

The extent to which you perceive that you have succeeded or failed in fulfilling your need for social connection by throwing a party is determined by your mindset. With a growth mindset you might consider that you had done all you could (accessed your resourcefulness) to make the party a success, and resolve to enjoy your special night. With a fixed mindset you might conclude your friends were largely unreliable, that the evening was an unfortunate endurance test, and vow never to have a party again.

Your wisdom supports your resourcefulness

Your wisdom is a function of your experiences and learning through life. It therefore represents your knowledge and understanding of how the world works. Your wisdom is unique because no one else has experienced things the way you have in life.

Imagine yourself at work, whether you run your own business or are employed by an organisation...

Things aren't going well at work and you know you need to do something about it. You decide to start working harder, staying longer at the office and investing more time at work at the expense of time with your family. You might even invest money, perhaps in training or equipment, or you decide to go out at lunchtime and after work more frequently to socialise with your colleagues, boss or clients. You invest your health in your work.

To the extent that you are successful this can create positive feelings, but if it is at the expense of your personal relationships and long-term health there is a big question as to whether the investment is worth the return. If you feel these investments are not worth the cost or are ineffective you will experience an emotional reaction: anxiety, panic, stress, perhaps even a sense of worthlessness.

Our beliefs about the world and how it works are directly influenced by our experience of our perceived successes and failures and the way we respond to them.

Our wisdom allows us to apply our resourcefulness effectively, or not, in the world that we know. When we are not sure how to address the issues we face we might seek help and advice. This can take many forms: professional advisers such as coaches, counsellors or therapists, friends or family, even online forums. The question to ask yourself here is, do you go to people who affirm your beliefs about the world and your capabilities, or do you go to people who see the world differently to you? And can therefore offer you a different perspective and the opportunity to see other possibilities?

People can only give you advice based on their wisdom. We create gurus out of people we regard as being very wise in their areas of experience in the world and we are happy to seek their advice, but seeking advice is not the same as acting on it.

Earlier in this chapter I wrote about the application of Newton's laws to our lives: 'To every action there is an equal and opposite reaction.'

This law represents our in-built resistance to learning that we all possess. Freud referred to it as our ego. Maxwell Maltz, author of *Psycho-Cybernetics*, referred to it as our self-image. Whatever you want to call it, it is the internal image you hold of yourself. When your brain perceives a threat to your internal image, and this can be anything that happens to you that runs counter to your entrenched beliefs, your brain will create a threat reaction, triggering one of the intrinsic responses of fight, flight or freeze.

It is only when you recognise this that you can overcome your evolutionary reactions and your natural resistance, so you can evolve your wisdom.

Exercise
Think about a time when someone offered you unwanted advice about how to deal with a difficult situation. How did you react? Did you listen to any of the advice or resist it?

When your wisdom can't support your needs

If we didn't believe that the world could satisfy our needs, there would be no point in living. Some people do reach this point and in its extreme manifestation they commit suicide. There are many who live in a state of resigned compliance, or as Henry David Thoreau put it, 'lives of quiet desperation'. Having given up hope they can fulfil their needs, they give up on their dreams and ambitions and just accept things the way they are.

When we don't feel that the world can fulfil our needs, feelings that life is futile, pointless or meaningless may be triggered. When these emerge our energy levels drop. What's the point of being energetic and enthusiastic if the world isn't going to fulfil your needs?

The spiritual perspective

Spiritual thinking is often dismissed by people because of its implied trust in forces outside of themselves. For those who are open, spirituality can help us to retain a healthy balance between control and uncertainty.

It is the acceptance of natural law that allows a spiritual dimension of life to emerge and develop.

A spiritual perspective on life allows you to let go of trying to control your circumstances and accept that the only control you can be sure of having in life is over your own thoughts and actions. You cannot control events or other people's responses to events; you can only control your own response to those events, and if you don't control your response then you are simply reacting to events. Whatever your perspective, your actions or reactions determine the course of future events. The process is woven together.

Respect for others

When we try and control other people to get our needs fulfilled we are committing a breach of trust. Napoleon Hill described the educated person as someone 'who has so developed the faculties of [their] mind that [they] may acquire anything [they] want, or its equivalent, without violating the rights of others.'

When we do not see the world as a place that can fulfil our needs, we look to control our environment and the people within it. This leads to frustration, anxieties and other negative emotions. You can test this on yourself if you have been in a controlling relationship, either as the controller or the controlled. Think back to a time when you felt out of control in a relationship and reconnect to your emotional state at that time.

In the workplace you might recognise this dynamic as the boss who surrounds herself with yes people but then holds them in contempt because of the control she has over them.

I once participated in a personal-development event during which I was asked to find a partner in the room and actively respect them.

Our partner was to stand in front of us and we had to kneel in front of them and bow down with our arms outstretched. While in this submissive position we had to stay there until we had fully accepted and respected the person for who they were, even though we might never have met them before. We then had to accept the experience in reverse as our partners respected us.

The tension in the room was palpable as we were challenged to move well outside our comfort zones and humble ourselves to a stranger.

My personal realisation came as a shock to my system as it brought home how little respect I had paid to most of the people in my life – and I include those closest to me. I had always thought of myself as a respectful person; what I came to realise from this exercise was that I had actually been a submissive person and this had led me to not respect those to whom I was submissive.

It is important to note that not respecting is not the same as disrespecting. To disrespect is to hold in contempt, and although I have met people who I did disrespect, for the most part I just had not given consideration to the fact that I was not giving people the respect they were due.

The upshot of this exercise was I determined that the future version of me would become a respectful person accepting of the fact that I did not know of the journey that anyone else was on and therefore could not and should not be passing judgements about them. This new perspective has had an amazing and unexpected side effect. The frustrations and irritations that I used to experience have largely disappeared.

Understanding that you have needs, accepting that your needs are very real and drive your behaviours, and then taking responsibility for fulfilling your needs in an appropriate fashion while believing that the world is abundant and has the potential to fulfil your needs, is a prerequisite for achieving your success and maintaining a peace of mind.

CREATING YOUR CENTRE OF GRAVITY

'To be yourself in a world that is constantly trying to make you something else is the greatest accomplishment.'

Ralph Waldo Emerson

Where our resourcefulness, needs and wisdom overlap we have the sweet spot, our centre of gravity, where it all comes together. This is where we effectively apply our resourcefulness to fulfil our needs using our wisdom to create the results we want. When it all comes together, we feel worthwhile as people. We feel fulfilled. We feel effective. This is when we experience feelings of success.

It all seems very simple and easy when it is presented like this, but life is never that simple. To experience your success, first you have to be able to envision it. Become conscious of what success looks like to you as an individual, and be able to follow the path to that success while staying open to the challenges and learning that you will face along the way.

You are on a journey, and how that journey unfolds is up to you. You cannot control all of the events that will happen along the way, and some of them may be very challenging, but you can choose how you respond to them and therefore how you influence the next series of events.

The journey you are on is the story of how you envision your success and develop your resourcefulness and wisdom to fulfil your needs successfully. It is your resourcefulness and wisdom that will help you navigate your journey when the challenges of life try to take you away from your vision of success.

Understanding your centre of gravity

Your centre of gravity is like a nuclear reactor. It is the source of almost limitless energy and power, if you know how to activate it and keep it topped up with the right fuel.

Your centre of gravity (COG) is the point where your resourcefulness, needs and wisdom overlap. It represents the point at which you are being most effective and getting the results you want from the investment of your resources.

You can always feel the pull of your centre of gravity.

The first thing to understand is that there is no such thing as neutrality. Your centre of gravity is either pushing you forwards or pulling you backwards. You will recognise the feelings of both.

When your COG is pushing you forward (positive) you feel excited and energetic about life. You feel like you can take on anything and you are happy to do so. The danger when you feel this strong is that you take on too much.

When your COG is pulling you back (negative) you feel lethargic and heavy. It takes a real effort of willpower to get going. You are likely to feel doubt and fear and perhaps feel that you are at your capacity of what you can cope with, and that any more and you will collapse under the weight.

If you do not feel either of those two extremes but more as if you are following a routine that you are happy to follow but it is neither a push or pull feeling – you might feel it is easy to get up, go to work and do what is necessary but there's just no spark – this is still a negative aspect of your COG.

Remember from the law of growth and decay. If you are not growing you are in a state of decay. It might be at the early stages and slow but there is no such thing as standing still.

Intuitively you will recognise the feeling of wanting to make your centre of gravity as big as possible. In simple terms: the more we can get our resourcefulness, needs and wisdom to overlap, the bigger our sweet spot will be and the more fulfilled, worthwhile and valuable we will feel. For example ...

I have been working with a client for sometime now. Let's call her client X. At the beginning she was full of doubts and concerns and uncertain about what the future held. From the beginning my objective was to get her to create her vision of the future for herself and her business.

As with most people I work with this was a challenge because it is not something we are ever really taught how to do. From the early days of school we are encouraged to think about what we want to do in life but we are never asked how we want to be, how we want to show up in the world.

As we worked together it was thrilling to see her vison become more concrete; as her feelings of resourcefulness grew, as her belief in her ability to fulfil her own needs grew and her awareness of the process and understanding the power of living to her values and of natural law all came together.

This is still work in progress for client X and your vision for your life will always be so, but the best I can offer you is a snippet from an email client X sent to me after one of our meetings.

'It's not easy to convey in words how much I have appreciated the sessions we have had and I feel this is mainly because, now that I look back on it all, I have found the help and support over the last months quite frankly overwhelming. Particularly when I look back at the changes you have helped me to manage. More noticeable is the change I see in myself – I feel like a different person. One with more confidence to go for it! I am much more likely to recognise opportunity rather than threat (for the most part anyway) and I understand more about why I am feeling a certain way and how to manage my thoughts and behaviours consciously, which is very powerful – I feel like I am finding myself and appreciating myself and my values and finally feeling comfortable that being me is ok.'

An amazing thing starts to happen when you realise your ability to enlarge your centre of gravity. You feel more empowered in all aspects of your life. You start to feel more resourceful. You may feel able to learn new skills, to put yourself in situations you might have avoided in the past. You also start to feel the emergence of new needs: what was satisfying enough before doesn't feel as satisfying any more. This is not the empty desire borne of longing, when you hope for a change in your luck. It is the result of the growth in your resourcefulness. The more you realise you can do, the more you want to do. This is the manifestation of the 'use it or lose it' principle. When you use your resourcefulness effectively you reinforce positive neural pathways in your brain and create new neural paths, which with practice and repetition become your new skills and habits.

Your wisdom grows as you develop your understanding of the natural laws and your faith in the way they work behind the scenes, influencing the results you achieve.

This becomes a self-powering process. The better the results you achieve in your life the more resourceful you feel, the more you are able to fulfil and satisfy your natural needs and the better understanding you develop of the world and your wisdom.

This is personal growth encapsulated in a simple model.

I was asked to work with client Z. When I met them for the first time I met a person so lacking in self-belief and confidence that it was difficult to understand how they were holding down their position in life.

What emerged was a tale of huge sadness; of a difficult childhood that had implanted a belief system in the client's mind that they were not worthy or capable of experiencing real success in their life. But this was not a victim mentality. The person I met with was not someone who felt sorry for themselves, but it was clear to me that they had no idea how to get themselves out of the entrenched thinking that was keeping them stuck in a desperation mindset.

It soon became clear that this client was someone of intelligence but who had never been given the encouragement to believe in it and do anything with it.

My challenge was to show client Z the windows into their resourcefulness, into the richness of their needs and to the inherent wisdom they held, but it would take the client's courage to open themselves up to the possibilities and to allow themselves to see the window. And that is exactly what they did.

As a result client Z has stepped up and into a new life with possibilities they couldn't conceive of when we first started working together

The reverse process is also true. There is no such thing as stasis, because whether we like it or not the world is always changing. So if you don't continue to fuel your personal growth, your centre of gravity starts to shrink. This means that you will start to feel less resourceful, unable to fulfil your needs and your view of the world as a place capable of fulfilling your needs starts to erode. Your self-confidence starts to ebb away and you begin to build a self-fulfilling circle of inactivity.

It is not a coincidence that we refer to highly successful people, in any walk of life, as stars. The stars in the universe are radiators of energy. They create massive amount of the stuff and send it out to illuminate the world. When you make the connection between your resourcefulness, needs and wisdom and create your vision of success so that you can plot your journey, you become a star too, creating a level of energy that is admired by others.

Exercise

Think about some of the people in your life. Now that you are more aware of this process, can you see it working in some of those people? Can you imagine it within yourself? Have you experienced it?

What gets in the way?

A growth mindset will enable you to develop your resourcefulness with inevitable positive consequences on your ability to fulfil your needs, develop your wisdom and consciously create your centre of gravity. A fixed mindset will keep you fixed in the cycle of thinking you developed as a child and transferred to the adult world. But the adult world is an unforgiving place. Parents and teachers are no longer there to encourage your learning and growth. Employers expect to train you in the ways of their specific operations, but beyond that they expect you to bring your resourcefulness and wisdom and apply them fully in the way you go about your work.

Burn-out is a common symptom of the modern workplace. It is the result of having to call on your energy reserves to drive you forward when you don't feel resourceful and aren't fulfilling your needs effectively. Its symptoms are exhaustion, lack of enthusiasm and motivation, frustration and cynicism, and as a result reduced effectiveness in every aspect of life.

Many organisations actively encourage this mad cycle. They work on the principle that if you're not stressed and worn out, then you are not working hard enough. The idea that work should be fun, enjoyable and rewarding is only accepted by a few organisations. Many people feel they need to wear their stress and fatigue on their sleeves as a sign of how committed they are and how hard they are working.

I'm a fan of the writings of Seth Godin. In one of his famously short blog posts he wrote 'nobody cares how hard you work'. This is a sad fact but true. What people care about is what you achieve. In the long run the only way to realise your potential is to understand your centre of gravity and to keep it growing. Misdirecting the way you apply your resourcefulness, failing to satisfy your needs, and ignoring the natural laws, is a recipe for disaster that will create negativity in your centre of gravity and more stress in your life.

Age is no barrier

For many, the period between fifty and sixty-five is about trying to survive before they get to the safety of retirement. Despite laws against age discrimination there is always a natural bias towards younger people when it comes to most jobs because of the assumption that younger people have more energy and are generally hungrier, and are therefore willing to work harder and longer to achieve the results the organisation wants. While human biology slows down with age, *you do not lose the ability to be energy-generating as you grow older.* It is possible to see young adults in their early twenties showing the symptoms of burn-out because they are not working in their natural area of creative expression. Equally there are middle-and older-aged people who have maintained their growth mindset and are as able to access their resourcefulness as they were in their younger years. These people don't want to fade out in their twilight years.

My experience of watching my father descend into a totally unresourceful state as the result of a conscious decision he took to withdraw from an active, intellectually stimulating life, has been hugely influential in the formulation of my thinking.

My father was a natural salesman with a gift for business but he found it stressful. As he climbed the corporate ladder, the responsibility of running companies with hundreds of employees weighed heavily on his shoulders. He had his first heart attack aged forty-four, the result of a combination of smoking, drinking and living in a constant state of stress. In 1976 he was awarded the MBE for his services to industry at Buckingham Palace: a very proud moment for the family. In 1986, at the age of fifty-three, following his third heart attack, he decided to take early retirement. I will always remember his words, 'Thank God I don't have to do that any more.' A lifetime of hard work and massive achievement captured in the most negative sentiment I had ever heard.

Over the next twenty years I observed this previously vital man withdraw from life as he followed his path of 'not doing'. His health and mental attitude continued to deteriorate. It seemed he had given up on life and we watched helplessly as life gave up on him.

Our appeals for him to be more active fell on deaf ears and we watched in frustration as his circle of friends dwindled. Eventually he became housebound while my mother's frustrations with him grew, and at the age of seventy she talked seriously to me about the possibility of leaving him. By now he was spending most of his time in front of the television watching ever more banal programmes for longer each day, my mum in the kitchen reading and listening to music, unable to bear being in the same room as her husband. She wanted to spend her twilight years travelling and making up for those years dedicated to raising me and two brothers. She wanted to see the world and experience different ways of living, and the great irony was that they had the money to do it – my dad's financial acumen had made sure of that. But he wouldn't spend it. He even denied himself one of his greatest pleasures, dining out.

My father had stopped the process of growth. His fears stopped him from imagining a future beyond his immediate circumstances and as this became reality and he lost his self-confidence, his vision of life became smaller and smaller.

My mum's death from an aggressive cancer hit Dad hard. He had depended on her for forty-nine years; celebrating his lack of competence in domestic matters and leaving the chores to her. Five years later my brothers and I watched a man who had achieved some great things in his life finally dwindle into nothingness. As I sat holding his hand in the nursing home in which he spent his last few weeks, I felt the deepest sadness I had ever felt in my life. By now his progressive kidney failure had taken away his sanity.

I saw my father become ever more fearful of life and give up his resourcefulness skill by skill. I vowed that I would never give up on mine. In my father's passing came my purpose: to understand how anyone can lead a purposeful and meaningful life.

Whatever your age, whatever your circumstances, understanding the way your resourcefulness, needs and wisdom interact will help you to do this. It gives you a process to follow and a way to understand your journey that will help you overcome the natural fears that will be triggered as you continue on the path of developing your resourcefulness, fulfilling your needs and growing your wisdom. Remember, if you move away from a growth mindset the natural processes of brain plasticity will cause you to lose neural connection and over time, you will become less resourceful. But if you use your brain, you develop new neural pathways and you become more resourceful.

I end this chapter with thoughts from four of the most successful people of the last 150 years.

'The only real mistake is the one from which we learn nothing.'
'One of the greatest discoveries a person makes, one of their great surprises, is to find they can do what they were afraid they couldn't do.'
Henry Ford

'I am enough of an artist to draw freely upon my imagination. Imagination is more important than knowledge. Knowledge is limited. Imagination encircles the world.'
'Life is like riding a bicycle. To keep your balance, you must keep moving.'
Albert Einstein

'Always do what you are afraid to do.'
'Dare to live the life you have dreamed for yourself. Go forward and make your dreams come true.'
Ralph Waldo Emerson

'Don't let the noise of others' opinions drown out your own inner voice.'
'Have the courage to follow your heart and intuition. They somehow already know what you truly want to become. Everything else is secondary.'
Steve Jobs

RENEW

'Becoming is better than being.'

Carol Dweck

Your centre of gravity determines what you will attract into your life.

There are two elements that control the path of your life: internal forces and external forces. External forces in which you play absolutely no part such as earthquakes, tornados, car accidents, bereavements, can change the course of your life and in some tragic cases will even end lives. These forces can only change the direction in which your life goes, but they do not control the journey that you then choose to follow. This is determined purely by the internal forces that exist inside you.

Viktor Frankl discovered in Auschwitz that freedom lies in the ability to choose your response to the world, whatever your circumstances. However limited your circumstances may seem, the reason people do not fulfil their potential and satisfy their needs is because they are unable to create a vision for their future. This ability is shaped from a very early age. In her research, that led to the idea of the fixed and growth mindsets, Carol Dweck made a wonderful but terrible discovery. She took groups of equally achieving children and allocated them to different teachers. In one of the sets the teachers were told that children were very gifted high achievers, and the teachers for the other groups were told that they were not very bright and were not likely to do well. The results were astounding. The first groups, where the teachers had been told the children were high achievers, started to achieve at a higher level than expected and the groups where the teachers were told the children were underachievers, started to perform at a level below that which was expected.

This experiment showed that it was the expectations of the teachers that had the major effect on what the students went on to achieve.

Remember Henry Ford's famous quote: 'Whether you think you can or you can't you're right'?

Think about what this means for you and your family: your ability to create a vision for your future is inextricably linked to the way you feel about your capabilities. Your belief about your capabilities stems from how resourceful you believe you are.

It has long been acknowledged that the circumstances into which you are born have a major impact on the shape and direction your life takes. And of course you had no choice in the matter of your birth and heritage. It was an act of random chance, but you are here and surely you want to make the best of it. Being born into a wealthy, educated, stable family is proven to give children a statistically better chance of success, but it is not a guarantee, just as being born into an impoverished household is not a sentence to an impoverished life.

Whatever start you have in life, once in adulthood it is up to you and how you think that determines the results you achieve.

If you come from a poor family, or if you have suffered a life-changing injury or a sudden loss, or if you were born with a disability, it is going to shape the way you think. But there are many examples of people who have not been constrained by the shackles of their thinking. They have cast off the limitations of their circumstance, upbringing, education and physical disability to become amazingly successful. Here's a list of just a few:

- Franklin D Roosevelt – polio
- Stephen Hawking – motor neurone disease
- Charlie Chaplin – from extreme childhood poverty to the most powerful man in the film industry
- Lee Trevino – born into poverty, became one of the greatest golfers in history
- Helen Keller – struck deaf and blind at nineteen months and became a novelist and campaigner.

Thinking about your centre of gravity

I have asked many people to create their centre of gravity statement and none of them has found it comfortable or easy to begin with. That's because your centre of gravity statement is about *how you want to feel about your life*, rather than what you want your life to be. For example, I want to feel that my life is full of possibility and I am maximising all my opportunities.

Most self-help programmes set your internal focus on listing your goals. Renew sets your internal focus on what you want to give to the world, rather than what you want to get from it. Knowing WHAT you want to be sets the milestones that you have to achieve by certain stages of life; I want to get you thinking about HOW you want to be. This will help you to identify your need behind your goals.

Exercise

Take a pen and paper and find a quiet place to relax, make sure you have uninterrupted time and allow a state of mind to emerge in which you can imagine that you are in the place of your success.

Using the present tense, write down the things you can see in your vision, write down how you are feeling and who is there with you and they are feeling. Capture as much detail as you can. Your sentences should start " I am ..." or "She/He/It is ..."

Exercise

If your thoughts turn to having a bigger house with beautiful furniture and all the fixtures and fittings, ask yourself what is sitting behind that mental image? If it is the feeling that life will be easier and more enjoyable with those things in your life, then the way you want to be is feeling easier about life and enjoying it more. If you see yourself driving a fast sexy sports car, what is behind that image? Is it really the feeling of being powerful and sexy yourself? Whatever comes to mind, as you relax *your objective is to understand the feeling behind the image.*

Your centre of gravity comes from visualising your ideal future, and interpreting the need behind it. If you can do this with ease then you can jump ahead. If you are finding it difficult, read on here.

Internal programming

Beliefs that were instilled into you at a very early age can still drive your behaviours and emotions at a much later stage of life. For example, you may have been told not to be a day dreamer, to be realistic, or that life's never going to be fair.

If you're finding it difficult to let your mind imagine your goals, of how you want your life to be, your beliefs could be stopping you.

Exercise

Write down the beliefs you hold about dreaming.

Now, add how you feel these beliefs are serving you now; are they help-ing you to move forward or are they keeping you stuck where you are?

Fears

When you allow your imagination to consider the way you would like your life to be, your brain's natural instinct may trigger a sense of fear.

You might recognise some of the following statements:

These things don't happen for people like me. This is a fear based on your sense of self-worth. Somewhere in your past you've developed the thinking that you will never be a success.

I have to be in control. Dreaming and imagining can create feelings of being out of control, so you limit what you do in order to stay in control.

I can't trust myself. The belief that even if you could live the life you want, you wouldn't be able to maintain it.

I don't have it in me. This is the idea that you don't have the resourceful-ness within you to create your dream.

The world doesn't work that way. You've never experienced the universe al-lowing your dreams to come true, so why should you trust it to deliver now?

Our fears can stop us from moving towards our dreams as our brain tries to protect us in case we get hurt by not achieving them. But your dreams will stay with you and reveal themselves in those moments of quiet reflection we all have.

It is no coincidence that Bronnie Ware discovered that the most com-mon and biggest regret people had in their last days was that they hadn't been true to themselves and their dreams.

Overcoming your internal programming and your fears

We tend to think of education and training as the acquiring of knowledge and skills, but a huge part of the process is overcoming our fears and beliefs. Overcoming your limiting beliefs and fears comes from having a growth mindset and accepting that you have the potential of infinite resourcefulness *throughout* your life.

When you create a vision for your centre of gravity, it will trigger your limiting beliefs and your fears because you are creating a vision that does not exist now and that you cannot achieve as the person you currently are. You can only achieve your vision by developing and growing into the person who can achieve the vision.

Remember, your vision exists beyond your current comfort zone.

The five keys to creating your centre of gravity

These are:

1. Curiosity
2. Forgiveness
3. Gratitude
4. Love
5. Courage

Curiosity

Too often I meet people whose minds are so closed that I sense they will never open up to the possibilities and opportunities that exist for them. They are so inflexible that it is not even worth getting into a conversation with them about it. I used to want to try and convince them but soon came to see the folly of this approach. The ideas and concepts put forward here represent a certain level of energetic vibration. If you are not on that vibration, you will not feel the possibility in life. In order to be able to do so, you have to adopt your growth mindset and ignite your desire to learn by activating your curiosity.

So the challenge now is: what does it take to change your vibration level? It is the power of 'what if'.

'What if' is a state of mind, and it is one of the biggest differentiators between the way a child and an adult think. Children have endless curiosity. I promised myself that when my kids started to question me about life I would always answer honestly and openly, but when they started asking 'why?' in the way that only children can, it only took a few months before I uttered those dreadful words 'because I said so'.

The sadness is that as we grow up we tend to have our curiosity knocked out of us. We are taught to stop asking WHY and start answering HOW. The world of academia is the world of WHY but in the business world the management mantra is 'don't bring me problems, bring me solutions'. As we progress through the various stages of life, we move from a state of curiosity to a state of knowing. Part of getting older is an assumption that we now know the answers to the challenges of life. Family and friends may turn to us for guidance when they aren't sure what to do. But at work we are paid to know what to do.

I know I share the feelings of frustration of many parents whose support has been rejected by their children who would rather struggle through on their own. But this is all part of the process of them developing their resourcefulness. The most important role you can play is to help them learn the lessons from their experience that will then help them to expand their resourcefulness, and show them how to develop and maintain a growth mindset.

Curiosity is maintained by understanding the power of WHAT IF and asking WHY NOT?

These qualities are the signature of a growth mindset and the key to raising your vibration level.

In his book *Power vs Force*, David Hawkins claims that people do not change their vibration level through their life by more than 5 per cent. I disagree. I believe that changing your vibration level is an act of intention. If you can develop a growth mindset, your changing vibration level is a fundamental part of your journey as you proceed along the path of creating your centre of gravity.

Forgiveness

The second key to growing your centre of gravity is forgiveness. You will remember that *The Thinking Revolution* is influenced by the work of Carl Jung. Remember his words: 'There is no coming to consciousness without pain.'

Growth is a painful process. As we grow in puberty we experience physical growing pains as our body changes. Our minds experience the same phenomenon throughout our lives. These may manifest as feelings of regret, inadequacy, grief, anguish, annoyance – the list is endless.

Coming to consciousness is the process of developing self-awareness. The difficulty with this process as we grow in self-awareness is that the learning always seems obvious once we know it, and it can be painful to realise that the answer was staring us in the face all the time. But this is the process of coming to consciousness.

This is why forgiveness is the second key to creating your centre of gravity. If you can't forgive yourself, your emotional reactions will affect what happens next by keeping you anchored in regret or blame. If you don't make the unconscious conscious, it will direct your life and you will call it fate. Coming to consciousness will inevitably cause you some pain as you have to deal with memories when you did not handle situations in the best way you could have done, and the consequences of that.

Forgiveness – the only path to helping you learn the lessons from these experiences – will develop your resourcefulness and help you to not repeat the same mistake again.

There will be times when coming to consciousness brings to your mind things that you have done when well, and then you can celebrate the skills and qualities you brought to the situation to bring about these great results. Remember to celebrate these memories. The process of coming to consciousness is just as important in the positive context because it is the process by which we learn how to recreate success. Too often something happens for the good and we take it for granted or dismiss it as luck because we don't realise the role we played in the process and then we can't recreate our success.

I'm sure you will have met, as I have, those self-effacing people who cannot accept the part they played in creating a successful experience. This is just as limiting to growth as being unaware of any negative behaviours that are leading to failure.

Most of us have been programmed to be modest from a young age, and being accepting of our abilities can feel uncomfortable. But denial of your abilities will stop you developing and creating your centre of gravity just as surely as not being able to forgive yourself for the ignorance of your unconscious negative behaviours.

I have learned that you cannot truly forgive others until you have learned how to forgive yourself. In forgiving yourself and overcoming the pain of developing your self-awareness and coming to consciousness, you come to realise that everyone else is going through the same process as you, albeit in a different time frame, and it then becomes easier to forgive others as well.

Gratitude

Being thankful is another pillar of spiritual and religious teaching. It is formalised in rituals such as Thanksgiving and Christmas and is the third key to creating your centre. It is your gratitude that determines whether you maintain an open mind or not.

Imagine this situation: you are at work, tasked with getting an important project finished by Wednesday afternoon. To achieve this you have been required to bring a number of different people together and coordinate their work towards the completion of the project. Then you discover that one of your team members, Silvie, hasn't actioned the printing of a brochure that has to be sent to key clients and therefore you are not going to achieve the Wednesday afternoon deadline. You look back at your notes: your instruction is clearly there in the minutes of the meetings which were distributed to everyone concerned.

But it's your neck on the line not theirs.

You now have some options: go into panic mode, blame Silvie for her incompetence, get on the phone to the printers to beg them for help, go to see your boss and come clean. In this moment it is going to feel difficult to feel grateful for this experience, but if you want to learn its valuable lessons then you have to get yourself to a place of gratitude. The only thing that you now have control over is the way in which you respond. Remember Viktor Frankl's lesson: 'Between stimulus and response, there is a space. In that space is our power to choose our response. In our response lies our growth and our freedom.'

It is your state of gratitude that allows you to move from an emotional reaction to a considered response. With this in mind, how could you respond to this mini-crisis at work with gratitude?

The reality is that, in this example, gratitude is likely only to be something that you can show after the event. On reflecting you will be able to see some lessons that can be learned. One lesson might be to reflect on what you could have done differently to manage the project more effectively. Without the practice of gratitude the strong probability is that Sylvie would be reprimanded in some way.

One difficult situation I had to deal with as a manager was when two salespeople I managed had been overstating their sales figures fraudulently to achieve their targets. The outcome of my investigation resulted in them both being disciplined and given a formal warning. Their responses were indicative of people who could not be grateful for the experience. One went on long-term sickness claiming discrimination and one launched a claim for constructive dismissal.

Both lost their cases and ended up leaving the company. In the process they also lost friendships and the respect of other managers who had helped them progress through their careers.

If they had been able to practice gratitude for their experience and seen it as a growth opportunity the outcome would have been very different for everyone involved.

Think of the times when you have been hurt by a moment of inconsideration from your husband or wife, or a friend unwittingly made you feel small, or you felt the frustration of dealing with children who won't eat the tea you spent time cooking for them.

Why should you be grateful for these experiences? There are three reasons why you should maintain a state of gratitude:

1. We've all experienced the withering putdown: 'I'm not angry, I'm just disappointed'. Negative emotions like anger, resentment and disappointment close off the opportunity for discussion and are an obstacle to openness between people and a healthy sense of personal responsibility. If you feel upset or angry by someone's behaviour, remember that you are experiencing a negative emotion. You can't erase the emotion, but you can choose to see the bigger picture by being grateful for the experience.

2. Gratitude is good for the brain. Scientists using FMRI scanning techniques have been able to show that the practice of gratitude increases activity and blood flow in areas of the brain such as the hypothalamus, which produces many of the feel-good hormones. In accordance with the brain's natural plasticity, regular practice of gratitude will cause the areas of the brain associated with positive emotions and feelings to become more active, while those associated with negative feelings and emotions will be weakened, creating a more positive balance.

3. Gratitude is good for your psychological well being. Researchers have shown that people who actively practise gratitude show more determination, perseverance, tolerance, attention and enthusiasm than those who don't.

As you progress on your journey, the practice of gratitude will reward you in many ways, not least of which is to keep your mind open to learning the valuable lessons from your experiences.

Exercise

To activate your gratitude, as you lie on your bed before you go to sleep, think of five things that happened during the day for which you can be grateful.

They can be small and seemingly insignificant: sometimes I'm thankful for seeing birds flitting about in the trees outside my apartment. They can be big events like winning a competition or getting a pay rise. And if something bad or irritating has happened, be grateful for that as well. Your learning comes from developing your resourcefulness to handle the things that go wrong in life as much as the things that go well.

You will be surprised how your view of life changes if you follow this practice regularly.

Love

By love I am referring to our love for humanity. In our day-to-day lives we sometimes act in ways that are unlovable and we certainly have dealings with people who do things that are unlovable.

Here are just a few examples of unlovable behaviour: Ignoring someone, deliberately triggering an emotional reaction in retaliation for a perceived hurt, showing a lack of consideration or a lack of empathy, undermining rather than supporting your partner.

If you want to be loved, you have to be loving in your own nature.

Love is an aspect of our emotional state and our emotional state shows up in our body language. It comes through in the micro-muscular movements of the face, the pace of breathing, our heart rate and posture, and there is very little you can do about it. If you've ever watched high-stakes poker games you will have seen how the players wear all sorts of devices – sunglasses, hats, masks – to hide the micro-signals of their unconscious facial movements from their opponents.

We are very sensitive to these micro-signals and the only way to control them is through your emotional state. When you come from a state of love for humanity, your facial muscles and vocal chords reflect this and this changes the way you look and how you sound when you talk.

Withdrawing love is the most common form of punishment we dole out to the people in our lives. It is very potent and sends out a very clear message, without having to say a word. Instinctively we know the withdrawal of love is a very powerful emotional punishment. This can lead us to feeling guilt and wanting to offer it back. This might be in the form of a hug or some other form of appropriate physical contact if it's in the workplace, like a handshake or the touching of an arm. But in this move the power now moves to the other person and they can accept or reject your offer of love. If they accept it you feel redeemed, but if they don't, the cycle starts up again. To avoid the power games that go with the giving and withholding of love there is only one answer: to always be in love with humanity and to give your love freely without expecting anything in return.

Love is the most powerful source of energy we have at our disposal and is the most misunderstood.

Passive aggression and vulnerability:

The withholding of love is recognised as passive aggression. You make judgements about people within micro-seconds of meeting them and they do of you. In these instants you will have made a judgement about whether you think they are loving or not, although it's more likely to be an unconscious thought about them seeming hard, soft, genuine or interested. And in that moment of judgement you have unconsciously decided how you are going to respond to them. This is an act of self-defence, because to be open and loving when the other person isn't leaves you vulnerable to the hurt of love being withheld.

One of the most watched TED talks is Brené Brown on the power of vulnerability with over nearly 25 million views (*https://www.ted.com/talks/brene_brown_on_vulnerability*). In simple terms, vulnerability is the giving of love irrespective of whether you receive any in return. In her talk Brené shows us how showing our vulnerability is an expression of love because it takes trust. When we offer our vulnerability to someone we are showing that we trust and that we have the self-belief to be able to deal with any attack on it.

Courage

It takes courage to offer love when it is not being offered in return.

It takes courage to show gratitude for events and experiences that have hurt you.

It takes courage to offer forgiveness to yourself and others for that hurt.

It takes courage to activate your curiosity and open yourself to the possibility that the beliefs you hold to be true about yourself and the world might, in fact, not be true.

You will see that by using the five keys you are opening the doors to uncertainty:

- Curiosity takes away the certainty of what you know.
- Forgiveness takes away the certainty of being right and wrong.
- Gratitude takes away your certainty of what is positive and negative.
- Love takes away your certainty of what is good and bad.
- Courage gives you the fortitude to live with uncertainty.

Becoming intentional about your centre of gravity

The law of intention states that you will not achieve your ambitions unless you have a specific intention to make them happen. This is why, for so many people, ambitions remain as dreams rather than reality.

Remember that your centre of gravity is the point where your resourcefulness, needs and wisdom intersect, and your journey is the path you travel to create your centre of gravity. If you do not take an intentional approach to this, your life will evolve and you will have little influence on the direction it takes. A lack of intention is responsible for the feeling of disempowerment and disengagement that so many people feel today.

In the absence of intention, your unconscious mind fills your centre of gravity with your unconsciously held vision of the world. If you are lucky it will be a vision that is positive and will carry you forward and if you are unlucky it will be a vision constructed from all your negative experiences. Your centre of gravity cannot remain empty. It is like a vacuum, a space devoid of matter, and nature does not allow vacuums to exist.

There is a truth to be learned: what you hold in your centre of gravity will always come to fruition in your life.

I would like to offer you two personal examples of the power of your centre of gravity. The first is still painful to me and I'm shaking as I write.

After my marriage had broken down and I had moved away from the family home for the first time, I had the space and the time to reflect on my role in the break-up. There was a truth that I had to face up to.

My ex-wife was the most beautiful and charismatic woman I had ever known. She was the sort who would turn heads when she walked into a room; and even though I knew she loved me and I for sure loved her, underlying was a deep insecurity that I was not worthy of her.

For all the years that I had the high status and high-paying job I was able to ignore my insecurity, but when those symbols of success went, slowly but surely the insecurity rose to the surface.

Through all the years of my marriage it was the feeling of unworthiness that formed my centre of gravity and it wasn't just in relation to my wife. It was how I felt about my career as well.

As I put the pieces together I could see how this fear had eroded my self-confidence and eaten into the trust that had underpinned the marriage in the early years.

But here's the thing: I had no idea at the time. I thought I was doing all the right things working harder to maintain the façade rather than working on my mindset and ensuring that my centre of gravity was populated with the vision of the future that I truly wanted rather than by the fears and negative beliefs held in my subconscious.

Now come forward with me to April 2012. I've just been made redundant for the second time. I have that feeling that so many people describe when they've experienced the same. A feeling of freedom and the opportunity to finally do something of meaning with my life. It feels exciting and very scary at the same time, a bit like being at the top of the roller-coaster ride as you wait to go over the top and on the terrifying drop to the first stomach-wrenching twist in the track.

But this time I know what I want, I've created a vision. I have consciously populated my centre of gravity with a detailed picture of how I want my life to be. The only trouble is I have no idea how I'm going to achieve it.

Come forward with me again to March 2016.

I've just finished the manuscript to my third book (this one), something that I would never have imagined before. I have created a personal-development business that delivers both live and digital training and I have also become a motivational speaker.

But most importantly, I have developed a relationship with my children that is stronger than ever before.

And yes, this was the vision that I installed in my centre of gravity.

The power of visualisation

As far as we know visualisation is a uniquely human skill. It is the ability to bring to our minds something that doesn't exist. As far as science can tell us, birds, mammals and insects start their seasonal migrations not because they imagine the coming change but because they sense it in their environment. Because we can imagine, we have built houses and societies that can support us in every environment the world has to offer. If we can do this at a social level, why are we so bad at doing it at an individual level?

George Bernard Shaw said: 'The reasonable man adapts himself to the world; the unreasonable one persists in trying to adapt the world to himself. Therefore, all progress depends on the unreasonable man.'

When you become a person with a vision, you will realise that you are creating something new in your life. It can be no other way. If it's not new, it's not a vision because it must already exist.

Do not be surprised if other people do not share your vision. This is only natural because your vision comes from your unique combination of resourcefulness, needs and wisdom. You need to be prepared for any resistance generated by your own fears and from others. This is when you will need your willpower.

The role of willpower

If our mental powers were athletes, willpower would be the 100-metre sprinter. Willpower enables you to hold your intention in your mind, but does not have the long-term staying power necessary to see you through to your goals.

Willpower comes into its own during short-term battles with your doubts and fears. Your doubts and fears will try and eat away at your vision if you allow them. They are guerrilla fighters, coming in undercover and taking pot shots.

Your willpower can hold your vision in the thinking part of the brain, the frontal cortex. It can prevent the emotions of fear and doubt generated in the limbic system from overpowering your vision, and allow your thinking brain to manifest the actions necessary to turn your thoughts into reality.

But it can only do this in short bursts. For long-term and sustained perseverance you must go beyond your willpower to your 'why'.

Your vision

Any goal worth aspiring to will have a long-term aspect and you will need something to hold you strong over the long term. This is your vision.

Your vision has to be created at such a level of detail that your imagination can see it as a complete picture. What is your motive for your ambition? Quite literally: Why do you want to achieve your vision? When you have a full and rich understanding of your 'why', all parts of your brain can do exactly what they have evolved to do best.

It is our vision that drives us forward with a real sense of purpose, it is our vision that helps us to see the learning in the setbacks we will encounter throughout our lives.

The Final Curtain

'And now, the end is near/And so I face the final curtain.'

It was Paul Anka who wrote those words and Frank Sinatra who made them immortal when he recorded the song.

I remember when it became a hit; I was eleven at the time and it has stuck with me for all these years. It is still one of my favourites, I think because I was starting to think about my future. I was about to move up to secondary school and life seemed to be getting serious.

Those words also resonated with a vision that had started to form inside me. It was a long dark tunnel and at the end of it was a bright light: it was the light of retirement.

It might seem unbelievable to you that my thoughts were already so formed at such an early age but that was how life seemed to me, a long dark tunnel that had be endured until the joy of the bright light was reached. And there were only two ways in which the end could be achieved: either through a lifetime working as an employee or by becoming rich enough that work could be given up and replaced by a life of non-work.

The vision of the dark tunnel guided my actions for many years and was the driving force for my ill-fated attempts to get out of the world of work and start my own businesses in an effort to become rich enough to escape.

I would be well into my fifties before I was to understand the poverty of that way of thinking and discover that there was a different way of looking at the world. A way of seeing the world that would blast away the tunnel and allow me to see the true scope and possibility of life in a way that hadn't been revealed to me before.

Why a revolution?

What I have discovered since then is that everyone has their own vision of their journey and that many people share the vision of life as some sort of endurance test that has to be got through before the joy can be realised. But I have also seen that many people don't see life that way. They see it as a journey to be revelled in and to be enjoyed along the way.

I'd love to know why my vision was so dark and gloomy but all I can say is that it must have been a consequence of my early experiences of life and the lessons I learned in those formative years: my programming.

This programming ran my life just like a computer programme determines what a computer does. And it takes someone to turn off the computer or for it to crash before it is rebooted and a new programme can run.

My reboot happened when my marriage broke down and I realised that if I didn't change my thinking I would end up repeating the patterns of living that had taken me to that point, and I knew I didn't want that to be the case.

That's the thing about programming; you don't know its running until it stops working for you. But here's the 'big thing': sometimes it's hard to see that your thinking is not serving you even when it is clear to other people.

That's why this book and my business is called *The Thinking Revolution*: because if you want to change the results you are getting in your life you have to change the way you think.

And to achieve that takes a revolution.

Change before you have to

The trouble with a revolution is that it is rarely orderly. It usually means there are some people who are happy with the status quo and some who are not; and when the level of dissatisfaction reaches boiling point the revolution occurs.

At the individual level the thing that likes the status quo is your brain, and as bizarre as it sounds it doesn't matter whether the status quo is positive or negative. Which is why many people hang on in quiet desperation before it literally gets too much to bear any longer.

But the good news is that there is a different way.

Empowered or victim?

It would take a senior executive at one of the companies I worked at to look me in the eye, and tell me to stop being a victim, for me to even realise that I was allowing events to direct my life and not the other way round; and it had been this way for my entire life. That was my status quo back then and my mind came up with every excuse as to why I couldn't do anything about it:

I was too old, hadn't been to the right school, didn't have the right qualifications. You name it, my brain came up with it as an excuse.

I wasn't even in control of my own thinking.

Science and spirituality are on your side

But science has come a long way since those days and we now know how powerful our emotions are and how they drive the way we think, even when we don't realise it. These advances in neuroscience and psychology have also opened the window to the tools and techniques we can use to wrest control of our thinking from our emotions, so that we can become empowered in our thoughts rather than victims of our emotions. The amazing thing is that these sciences are proving to be true the spiritual advice that has been around for 3,000 years and that has been available to anyone with the will to see it, hear it and act on it.

Success; the ultimate goal

My vision of success all those years ago was to get to the end of the tunnel, but what drives all of us is a sense that we have a seed of success inside.

For some people it is clear and obvious where their talents lie and therefore how they will achieve their success. We can think of stars like David Beckham, Nicola Benedetti, Damien Hirst or entrepreneurs like Richard Branson and Oprah Winfrey, who they have become successful by capitalising on their natural talents. But all of them had to overcome challenges and face failures and rejection along the way. Success doesn't come pain-free and this is where a lot of people drop out, because they don't want to fight through that pain barrier.

But many do not believe they have an obvious talent and this holds them back. They could do worse than take a leaf out of Will Smith's book.

'I've always considered myself to be just average talent but what I have is a ridiculous insane obsessiveness for practice and preparation.'

The tools to win

You were born with all the tools you need to achieve your intuitive success. The only thing that has got in the way is the programming you received in your formative years. If you are willing to let that go and replace it with a new way of thinking you can achieve the success you want.

Resourcefulness: These are your natural personal qualities that enable you to respond to any situation and get the best out of yourself in the moment. It is your resourcefulness that allows you to have infinite potential.

Needs: Your natural needs drive your motivation; becoming clear on the needs you are striving to fulfil and whether you are fulfilling them in the positive or the negative is part of your journey to self-awareness.

Wisdom: You have a wisdom which is made up of your values, beliefs and your relationship to natural law. Your values describe the things that you will or won't do. Your beliefs describe the things you think you can or can't do, and your relationship with natural law defines the way you approach the business of life.

Centre of Gravity: Your centre of gravity is the place where your resourcefulness, needs and wisdom come together. It exists in your mind and it drives your actions and behaviour. Your centre of gravity is like a magnet, attracting to you the physical manifestations of the thoughts you hold there. It cannot be a vacuum.

When you populate it with thoughts of the things you really want it will direct your mind to see those opportunities in the every day. It is then up to you, what you choose to do with the opportunity. If you do not consciously populate your centre of gravity with thoughts of things you want to create in your life, your unconscious mind will populate it with the limiting beliefs you hold to be true and these are what will become true for you in reality.

The Journey

Your journey began when you were born. In your formative years your parents and other adult influences governed the path you took, but you have been in control of your journey since becoming an adult.

But you have probably never had the journey explained to you and therefore could not see the opportunities that presented themselves along the way.

Now you know that the journey is predictable and that to appreciate and prosper from it you have to be prepared to be the hero of your journey.

The only questions that remain are: Have you heard your call to adventure? and Are you prepared to accept it?

The light at the end of the tunnel

The principles laid out in *The Thinking Revolution* are new but they are based on the deliberations of many thinkers through the centuries. They come from a line of thinking that values the human spirit for the creative force it is. I have been lucky enough to have people ask me to work with them and show them how to unleash the full power of their natural creativity so they can achieve their success. It has been a privilege to work with these people as clients and from that some have become friends.

I finally reached the light at the end of my tunnel a few years ago and thanks to the principles of *The Thinking Revolution* I discovered not a relief at the end of my working life but a new charge of energy and the thrill of the untapped potential that still lay within me. But more than that the will, determination and strength to want to make it real.

If you can take one thing from what you have read let it be that the law of perpetual transformation of energy is what brought this book into existence. It started off as a thought and now it is real.

You have the same power within you, to make your thoughts real.

I wish you all the luck in the world on your new journey to tap the potential that still lies within you.

Further Reading

BOOKS

Ariely, D (2009). *Predictably Irrational*. HarperCollins.

Baumeister, R F (2012). *Willpower*. Penguin.

Bobich, Dr Z (1999). *Recognise Your Enemy*. Dr Z Bobich.

Buckingham, M (2007). *Go Put Your Strengths to Work*. Free Press.

Burg, B & Mann, J D (2007). *The Go-Giver*. Penguin.

Byrne, R (2006). *The Secret*. Simon & Schuster.

Cain, S (2012). *Quiet*. Crown Publishing.

Campbell, J (2008). *The Hero with a Thousand Faces*. New World Library.

Canfield, J (1999). *Chicken Soup for the Soul*. Vermillion.

Chapman, G (2010). *The 5 Love Languages*. Northfield Publishing.

Chopra, D (1996). *The Seven Spiritual Laws of Success*. Bantam Press.

Covey, S (2004). *The 7 Habits of Highly Effective People*. Simon and Schuster.

Dweck, C (2012). *Mindset: How You Can Fulfil Your Potential*. Robinson.

Frankl, V E (2004). *Man's Search for Meaning: The classic tribute to hope from the Holocaust*. Rider.

Gardner, H (1993). *Multiple Intelligences: A New Horizon*. Fontana.

George, W (2003). *Authentic Leadership*. Jossey Bass.

Gladwell, M (2008). *Outliers*. Penguin.

Glover, R A (2003). *No More Mr Nice Guy*. Running Press.

Goleman, D (1996). *Emotional Intelligence*. Bloomsbury Publishing.

Greaves, J & Bradbury, T (2009). *Emotional Intelligence 2.0*. Talent Smart.

Griffin, J & Tyrrell, I (2013). *Human Givens*. HG Publishing.

Gyalwang, D (2012). *Everyday Enlightenment*. Penguin.

Hawkins, D R (2002). *Power vs Force*. Hay House.

Hill, N (2007). *Think and Grow Rich*. Wilder Publications.

Jeffers, S (2007). *Feel the Fear and Do It Anyway*. Vermillion.

Khaneman, D (2011). *Thinking, Fast and Slow*. Penguin.

Kübler-Ross, E (2014). *On Death and Dying*. Scribner.

Loehr, J & Schwartz, T (2003). *The Power of Full Engagement*. Free Press.

Maltz, M (2002). *Psycho-Cybernetics*. Prentice Hall Press.

Pink, D (2008). *A Whole New Mind*. Marshall Cavendish.

Rath, T (2007). *StrengthsFinder2.0*. Gallup Press.

Schwartz, B (2004). *The Paradox of Choice*. HarperCollins.

Scott Peck, M (2008). *The Road Less Travelled*. Ebury Publishing.

Seligman, M E P (2003). *Authentic Happiness: Using the New Positive Psychology to Realise your Potential for Lasting Fulfilment*. Free Press.

St John, R (2010). *The 8 Traits Successful People Have in Common: 8 to be Great*. Train of Thought Arts Inc.

Stuart, D (2013). *ResourcefulMe*. Callisto Green.

Waitzkin, J (2007). *The Art of Learning*. Free Press.

Ware, B (2011). *The Top Five Regrets of the Dying*. Hay House.

Wattles, W D (2010). *The Science of Getting Rich*. Capstone Publishing Ltd.

JOURNALS

Babiak, P, Hare, R, Neumann, C (2010). *Corporate psychopathy: Talking the walk*. Behavioral Sciences & the Law, Vol 28, Issue 2, March/April 2010: 174-193.

Chang, L-H, Shibata, K, Andersen, G J, Sasaki, Y, Watanabe, T (2014). *Age-Related Declines of Stability in Visual Perceptual Learning*. Current Biology, Vol 24, Issue 24, December 2014: 2926–2929.

Fulton, J F (1953). *The Limbic System: A Study of the Visceral Brain in Primates and Man*. Yale Journal of Biology and Medicine, Vol 26.

Kini, P, Wong, J, McInnis, S, Gabana, N, Brown, J W (2016). *The effects of gratitude expression on neural activity*. NeuroImage, Vol 128:1-10.

REPORTS

2014 Trends in Global Employee Engagement. Aon Hewitt.

Huppert, F A & So, T T C (2009). *What percentage of people in Europe are flourishing and what characterises them?* Well-Being Institute. University of Cambridge.

State of the Global Workforce. Gallup, 2013.

LINKS

http://www.scientificamerican.com/article/how-has-human-brain-evolved/

http://www.theglobeandmail.com/report-on-business/coming-saturday-the-inside-story-of-why-blackberry-is-failing/article14563602/
http://digest.bps.org.uk/2013/02/extreme-fear-experienced-without.html
http://www.utdallas.edu/~assmann/hcs6367/marinova_todd_marshall_snow00.pdf)
http://digest.bps.org.uk/2013/02/extreme-fear-experienced-without.html
http://www.chopra.com/the-law-of-giving-receiving
https://news.google.com/newspapers?nid=1454&dat=19630606&id=QURjAAAAIBAJ&sjid=PHQNAAAAIBAJ&pg=626,923072&hl=en
http://www.theguardian.com/society/2015/feb/22/youth-unemployment-jobless-figure
(www.bbc.co.uk/news/magazine-26384712).
https://en.wikipedia.org/wiki/Biorhythm
https://www.theguardian.com/science/2016/apr/10/neanderthals-may-have-died-of-diseases-carried-by-humans-from-africa
http://www.bbc.co.uk/news/science-environment-13874671
http://www.nytimes.com/1988/03/03/us/health-new-studies-report-health-dangers-of-repressing-emotional-turmoil.html
https://www.psychologytoday.com/blog/prefrontal-nudity/201211/the-grateful-brain

ACKNOWLEDGEMENTS

This book has only come together because of the help and support I have had from many people.

They are the people who have given me opportunity but also they have been prepared to tell me some difficult truths as well; from the tension of these two positions my thoughts were honed and focused and the result, at least for me as the author, is a much tighter and stronger book.

In no particular order, I would like to thank:

Pauline Herring: for taking the plunge and becoming my first client and giving me the opportunity to prove the value of my processes.

Nicole Speller: for becoming my second client and trusting in me as a source of counsel in challenging times.

Howard Scott: for believing in me twice. Firstly when he employed me as a newspaper publisher and secondly when he introduced me to David and Richard of OnePerformance.

David Palser and Richard Leech: for offering me challenges and opportunities to develop my skills in presenting and facilitation.

Ben Hart: for giving me his incredibly valuable time and advice.

Ian Dodds: for being so generous with his advice and experience and for his general support.

Clare Christian: for maintaining her patience and faith in me when things were definitely going off course.

And for countless other people whose willingness to listen and feedback to me added to the depth I was able to bring to the book.

ABOUT THE AUTHOR

Dene Stuart has over thirty years commercial, leadership and managementexperience, having held director roles within major national and regional media companies. Managing large teams in multi-site offices gave Dene the broadest possible range of employment, team, motivational and performance issues to deal with in the corporate world.

He has also started and managed several businesses of his own learning the issues of entrepreneurship and business ownership on the way.

However it was the life-changing events he met with in his personal life, overcoming Hodgkin's Lymphoma, coming through two career redundancies and finally the breakdown of his marriage that were the key to his interest in personal development and performance. These were the catalysts that led to him founding The Thinking Revolution.

Dene is an accredited professional in personality profiling and emotional intelligence and has a BSc in Management Science from The University of Manchester, Institute of Science and Technology. His first book *ResourcefulMe*, was published in June 2013 and *The Thinking Revolution* is his second book. His third book, *The Beginner's Guide to The Brain, The Mind and Thinking* will be published in early 2017.